Life and Practice in the Early Church

Life and Practice

in the

Early Church

A Documentary Reader

EDITED BY

Steven A. McKinion

New York University Press

New York and London

NEW YORK UNIVERSITY PRESS
New York and London

© 2001 by New York University
All rights reserved.

Library of Congress Cataloging-in-Publication Data
Life and practice in the early church : a documentary reader / edited by
Steven A. McKinion.
p.   cm.
Includes bibliographical references and index.
ISBN 0-8147-5649-2 (pbk. : alk. paper) —
ISBN 0-8147-5648-4 (cloth : alk paper)
1. Church—History of doctrines—Early church, ca. 30–600—Sources.
I. McKinion, Steven A. (Steven Alan)
BV598 .L54 2001
270.1—dc21   2001000564

New York University Press books are printed on acid-free paper,
and their binding materials are chosen for strength and durability.

Manufactured in the United States of America

10 9 8 7 6 5 4 3 2 1

To
Ginger, Lachlan, and Blakely

Contents

Acknowledgments

The completion of this project is due to the diligence and work of a number of individuals. I would like to offer my deepest appreciation to those who have contributed either directly or indirectly to the present work.

Professor Iain R. Torrance first inspired me to search the riches of the patristic writers, and for that I am grateful. His friendship has meant more to me than he will ever know. He is a mentor in the truest sense of the term.

I am thankful to President Paige Patterson and my colleagues at Southeastern Seminary for an environment in which scholarship is not divorced from the functional aspects of the Christianity. Along with academic freedom, there is an awareness of a responsibility to Christian service and pastoral concern. This may not be the garden of Eden, but it is close.

My students here at Southeastern are the real inspiration behind this text. Dialogue in class about these very topics has shaped its framework and direction. A "focus group" of students has been particularly helpful. John Nixon, Miles Mullin, Bob Olsen, and Keith Griffin have read every word and made comments that have strengthened the volume.

I cannot say enough about Jennifer Hammer, my editor at NYU Press. She has proven to be indispensable. Besides seeing something in the manuscript worth publishing, she made comments throughout the process that have made it worth reading. There is something of her contribution on nearly every page, and I am immensely grateful to her, along with the entire team at NYU.

I was fortunate to be reared in a home that demonstrated the importance of many of the themes in the selections that follow. My wife, Ginger, inspired me at every turn to press on with the project. She is a helpmate in every way. My children, Lachlan and Blakely, are too young (four and two, at this time) to know the influence they have on their father. I lovingly dedicate this volume to my wonderful family.

Steven A. McKinion
Wake Forest, North Carolina

Introduction

This collection of primary texts is intended to introduce the story of how the early Christians practiced their faith. It is not a survey of theology per se, but a survey of how theology was actually lived and played out by the community of faith called the Christian church. The selections that follow demonstrate how early believers "did church." They stand at the nexus of belief and practice, of theory and action, of theological and social history. They demonstrate variation and diversity regarding how faith was worked out in the patristic period.[1] The reader will discover many different ways in which Christians experienced and expressed their community of faith.

Why is a collection of this nature necessary? The question can be answered at two levels. On the philosophical level, early Christian writings reveal a great deal about the Christian tradition and the wider culture in which Christianity developed. On the practical level, most one-volume document collections tend to be concerned almost exclusively with theological issues and dogma, often to the neglect of more functional matters. Also, they frequently attempt to be "all things to all people," encompassing such a vast period of time that the selections must be brief. While there are many good collections, there are few works that provide substantial selections concerned exclusively with life and practice in the patristic period. This volume seeks to fill that void.

The selection of particular passages was guided by a few broad parameters. First, the documents date from the end of the first century C.E. to roughly the fifth century. This interval allowed for a wide range of developments to take place. Second, the writing must have articulated a widely accepted belief or practice, have been written by someone in a position of authority whose instruction would be given considerable weight in its original setting, or have challenged the prevailing position of the time. Third, the document from which the passage is taken must exist in a readily accessible English translation in order to allow the reader to follow up what is presented here. I have chosen to use documents from the Ante-Nicene Fathers (hereafter ANF) and the Nicene and Post-Nicene Fathers (hereafter

NPNF) series because of their availability in both printed and digital formats. It should be noted, however, that most of the translations presented in this volume have been altered slightly—and some considerably—by de-archaizing vocabulary (e.g., *thee* and *thou* to *you*) and by polishing some of the syntax. In places, what was deemed to be an inadequate translation has been replaced. This collection is not exhaustive (how massive that would be!) but is representative of the patristic writers.

Overarching all of the decisions has been a desire to broadly represent different traditions. Every Christian tradition is concerned with the subjects addressed in this book. While it would be tempting to extract only those passages affirming my own practice, it has not been my intention to do so. There are positions held by some of the Fathers that I would not affirm. The patristic writers were not monolithic in matters of life and practice, and it is important that the early Christians be heard in their own words and in the fullness of their diversity and their sometimes conflicting directives.

Doubtless there are texts omitted that many will consider indispensable, and others included that some would prefer to be absent. The material on the "cutting-room floor" is more voluminous that I had hoped. Too many important texts did not make the first, second, or subsequent cuts. However, decisions had to be made and important texts excluded. In the final analysis, each text here contributes in its own way to telling the story of life in the early Christian community.

The chapters are arranged to aid in telling this story. Chapter 1, "Entering the Community," examines the means by which one became a member of the church. The primary rite of initiation was baptism, which was usually preceded by a time of instruction in the Christian faith. While being prepared for baptism, the candidate was known as a catechumen. Not until after one's baptism would one be considered a fully participating member of the community.

The second chapter, "Assembling the Community," pictures the church at worship. Selections tell what occurred when the people assembled, and show what was expected of the worshippers before, during, and after the service itself.

The next two chapters are actually subsets of chapter 2. Within the services of worship, the people would be instructed in the Scriptures and would together participate in the Eucharist, or Lord's Supper. Chapter 3, "Instructing the Community," addresses teaching and preaching in the church, and chapter 4, "Uniting the Community," covers the ceremony of the Eucharist.

Chapter 5, "Expanding the Community," tells the story of the expansion of Christianity by various means of proclaiming the message of Jesus Christ. Christians won converts not simply by convincing them of the validity of their message through rhetorical means but by means of their moral living. In these selections, one finds numerous exhortations to believers to live properly in order to gain new members of the church.

The final chapter, "Leading the Community," shows how the church was organized for administering its various practices. The church was seen as analogous to a flock of sheep. "Shepherds" were responsible for guiding the flock, keeping it together, and protecting it from harm. Different offices developed to meet the various needs.

This text is intended for both graduate and undergraduate students, as well as pastors, laypersons, and interested observers. It requires little or no prior knowledge of Christian history or tradition. The activities of the early Christians are relevant for the social historian as well. Those interested in researching one or more of the themes addressed in the volume will find a starting place for further investigation.

It is hoped that these documents will together introduce the story of the early Christians. The reasons they give for doing things one particular way and not another, and for rejecting possible alternative practices are both illuminating and interesting. I trust that reading the words *of* the early Christian writers rather than words *about* the early Christian writers will enlighten the reader's understanding of life and practice in the early church.

ADDITIONAL READINGS

Altaner, B. *Patrology*, tr. H. C. Graef. Freiburg: Herder, 1960. 9th German ed. by A. Stuiber (Freiburg: Herder, 1980).

Baus, K. *From the Apostolic Community to Constantine*, ed. H. Jedin. New York: Seabury, 1965.

Baus, K., et al. *The Imperial Church from Constantine to the Early Middle Ages*, ed. H. Jedin. New York: Seabury, 1980.

Di Berardino, A., ed. *Encyclopedia of the Early Church*, tr. A. Walford. 2 vols. New York, Oxford University Press, 1992.

Ferguson, E., ed. *Encyclopedia of Early Christianity*. 2nd ed. New York: Garland, 1998.

Kelly, J. N. D. *Early Christian Doctrines*. 5th ed. New York: Harper and Row, 1978.

Pelikan, J. *The Christian Tradition.* Vol. 1, *The Emergence of the Catholic Tradition (100–600).* Chicago: University of Chicago Press, 1971.

Quasten, J., et al. *Patrology.* 4 vols. Westminster, MD: Christian Classics, 1953–1986.

Robinson, T. A. *The Early Church: An Annotated Bibliography of Literature in English.* Metuchen, NJ: Scarecrow, 1993.

CHAPTER I

Entering the Community

Baptism in the Early Church

⅊

Inherent in the continued existence of any community is the question of entrance. How is one to gain admission into the community? The rite of initiation for Christians has always been the ceremony of baptism with water. The English term "baptism" is a derivation of the Greek word *baptizo,* which means to immerse or to dip. It is one of a number of significant rites or ceremonies the Christians saw as indicative of their mission and message. These rites illustrated for the early Christians elements of the message they believed and preached. While the number of these practices varied from writer to writer and place to place, virtually all agreed on the importance of two in particular: baptism and the Eucharist, or Lord's Supper.[1] The church called these rites "sacraments," a term that comes through the Latin *sacramentum,* typically referring to an oath, which translated the Greek *mysterion,* meaning "mystery." They are also often termed "ordinances" of the church in many traditions.

Baptism and the Eucharist were both deemed important to the life of the community. The former was the means of initiation. The latter was a key component in the continued development of the believer and a central element in Christian worship. Christians believed that Christ himself had instituted these rites. His parting instruction to his disciples, referred to as the Great Commission,[2] was to baptize in the name of the Father, the Son, and the Holy Spirit. This command became the foundation for the church's practice of baptizing newly converted disciples. Moreover, Jesus' own baptism by John in the Jordan River served as an example of the rite of baptism, and was imitated by the early Christians.

5

Prior to baptism candidates for admission generally participated in a period of instruction. During this time catechumens, as they were called, learned the major tenets of the Christian faith and were examined with regard to their moral living. These catechumens were not considered fully participating members of the community. While they were expected to attend worship services with the other believers, they sat separate from them and were dismissed prior to the sharing of the Eucharist.[3] Often this time of training and testing would last up to a year, and sometimes longer. After the church had been convinced of the validity of the candidate's commitment to the community, baptism would be administered and the new initiate would participate in his or her first Lord's Supper.

In most cases baptism, which was also termed the bath of regeneration, consisted of immersing the candidate into water and anointing him or her with oil. Some writers allowed for baptism by affusion, or pouring water over the initiate's head. For the Christians, the act of baptism demonstrated a sharing in the death and resurrection of Jesus. Additionally, the rite represented the washing away of sin, and later was believed to effect it. Baptism was also a twofold seal or pledge between the initiate and the church, and the initiate and Christ. Often elaborate renunciations and professions were associated with the ceremony. The convert would renounce Satan and all his works, and confess Christ and his saving work. A commitment to faithfulness to the community and obedience to Christ was central to Christian baptism.

The emphasis associated with this rite gradually shifted from one of initiation into a community to a symbol of, or even a means of individual salvation. Initially, baptism was most important because it represented a decision to forsake sinful living, to obey the teachings of Jesus Christ, and to become a faithful member of the Christian community. As time passed, the importance of baptism became its effects on the individual, with a lessened focus on the community.

Another significant development in the administration of baptism was the baptism of infants. While there is little reference to such practice in the earliest Christian writings, and no explicit reference to it in the New Testament, there is little doubt that such a practice began quite early. One finds in Cyprian of Carthage an African synod's [gathering of important church leaders] decision to approve such a practice in the third century. The North African apologist Tertullian and Cappadocian Father Gregory of Nazianzus, writing in the third and fourth centuries, respectively, advised delaying baptism. However, even in the selections from those advocating delay, there is no prohibition of baptizing infants. In the fifth century, Latin theologian Augustine of Hippo firmly supported the practice.

The Didache (Early Second Century)

Didache is the Greek word for teaching, and is the shortened form of the full title of the work: *The Teaching of the Lord through the Twelve Apostles to the Nations.* Written anonymously in the first part of the second century, the *Didache* is part of the body of writings known as the Apostolic Fathers. As a church manual, its use and authority are seen in its circulation as well as its inclusion in a later work entitled *Apostolic Constitutions* as book seven. The fourth-century church historian Eusebius of Caesarea considered the work to be orthodox in its teaching but did not deem it appropriate to include it in the New Testament canon.[4] Athanasius of Alexandria regarded it as a useful tool for teaching catechumens.[5]

The instructions in the *Didache* demonstrate the diversity of practice vis-à-vis baptism. While the standard mode was immersion, pouring was allowed when running water was not available. That the wider congregation is encouraged to fast along with the initiates in preparation for the ceremony shows the relationship between baptism and entrance into the community of faith. Jesus' Great Commission is the obvious basis for the instruction to baptize using the Triune formula: in the name of the Father, Son, and Holy Spirit.

Chapter Seven

Concerning baptism, baptize in this manner: Baptize in the name of the Father, and of the Son, and of the Holy Spirit, in running water. However, if there is not running water, baptize in other water. If there is not cold water, then baptize in warm water. If there is neither cold nor warm, pour water three times over the head in the name of the Father and Son and Holy Spirit. Before the baptism let the one baptizing, the one being baptized, and others who can, fast. Instruct the one being baptized to fast one or two days before.

ANF 7, ed. A. Cleveland Coxe. Reprint, Peabody, MA: Hendrickson, 1994.

Justin Martyr (110–165)
First Apology

Justin is one of the most significant and well known of the second-century Christian apologists because of his defense of Christianity against Judaism and paganism. His conception of the *Logos* led him to conclude that the Greek writers were to the pagans what the Old Testament was to the Jews: a method of leading them to Christ. His *First Apology*, written in the middle of the second century, was intended to explain Christian belief and practice as a means of making the case for just and fair treatment of believers.

In this selection, Justin instructed baptism in the name of the Trinity and preparation of the candidate by prayer and fasting, similar to the *Didache*. The most significant instruction, however, was that the rite was reserved for those who had chosen to live according to the teachings of the community and had been forgiven of their past sins. This point explains why the Christians observed a period of training and instruction before granting admission to the church. The community would want to ensure that the candidate clearly understood its beliefs and practices. Additionally, the convert would benefit from extensive knowledge of the faith to which he or she had now subscribed. Justin perceived baptism as an act to be performed after one had determined to exhibit faithfulness to the faith of the community.

Chapter Sixty-One

I will also relate the manner in which we dedicated ourselves to God when we had been made new through Christ; knowing that, if we omit this, we seem to be unfair in the explanation we are making. As many as are persuaded and believe that what we teach and say is true, and undertake to live accordingly, are instructed to pray and to entreat God with fasting, for the remission of their sins that are past. We are to pray and fast with them. Then they are brought by us where there is water, and are regenerated in the same manner in which we ourselves were regenerated. For, in the name of God, the Father and Lord of the universe, and of our Savior Jesus Christ, and of the Holy Spirit, they then receive the washing with water. For Christ also said, "Unless you are born again, you shall not enter into the kingdom of heaven." That it is impossible for those who have once been born to enter into their mothers' wombs is clear to everyone. And how those who have sinned and repent shall escape their sins, is declared by Isaiah the prophet: "Wash yourself, make yourself clean; put away the evil of your doings from your souls; learn to do well; judge the fatherless, and plead for the widow: and come let us reason together, says the Lord. And though your sins are as scarlet, I will make them white like wool; and though they be as crimson, I will make them white as snow. But if you refuse and rebel, the sword shall devour you. The mouth of the Lord has spoken it."

We have learned from the apostles the following reason for this rite. We were born without our knowledge or choice by our parents coming together; and were brought up in bad habits and wicked training. However, in order that we may not remain the children of necessity and ignorance, but may become the children of choice and knowledge, and may obtain in the water the remission of sins formerly committed, there is pronounced over him who chooses to be born again, and has repented of his sins, the name of God the Father and the Lord of the universe. The one who leads the person that is to be washed to the bath is to call God by this name alone. For no one can utter the name of the ineffable God; and if any one dare to say that there is a name, he raves with a hopeless madness. And this washing is called illumination, because they who learn these things are illuminated in their understandings. In the name of Jesus Christ who was crucified under Pontius Pilate, and in the name of the Holy Spirit, who through the prophets foretold all things about Jesus, he who is illuminated is washed.

ANF 1, ed. A. Cleveland Coxe. Reprint, Peabody, MA: Hendrickson, 1994.

Tertullian of Carthage (160–212)

On Baptism

Tertullian was a North African apologist writing in the early third century whose primary opponents were the Gnostics, who considered the flesh to be evil and thus denied its salvation. Tertullian is often referred to as the founder of Western or Latin theology. He was one of the first major theologians and apologists to write in Latin.

In *On Baptism* Tertullian was writing against a woman named Quintilla, an anti-Christian who wished to denigrate Christianity. This was one of the earliest discussions of baptism, and the only treatise from before the pivotal First Ecumenical Council of Nicaea (A.D. 325) dedicated to the subject. It provides discussions concerning not only the rite itself but also its meaning and purpose.

In this selection Tertullian argued that the effects of baptism were all the more incredible because of the simplicity of the act itself. Where else might one imagine a person being immersed into water, sprinkled with oil, and afterward attaining eternal life? The author instructed that the minister should examine carefully those to be baptized, so as to avoid sharing in the sins of one who might fall into grave sin after baptism. Moreover, Tertullian advised the delay of baptism, especially for children. He expressed reluctance in advocating the baptism of infants. If children were initiated into the community through baptism, their adult sponsors—those who promised to teach these children the Christian faith—shared in the sins of those whom they pledged to instruct. In fact, he implied that children are innocent, and therefore not in need of baptism, demonstrating a view of the rite that emphasized its relationship to the church. Delay should also be exercised in the case of those who were unmarried. Temptation could be great, Tertullian argues, and initiates need to understand the gravity of their decision to be baptized. Each of these admonitions reveals his concern about those who would be considered a part of the community, and what post-baptismal sin might mean to the Christian witness of both the individual and the church.

The ceremony was preceded by preparation of the candidate through fasting, prayers, and the confession of past sins throughout the night prior to the baptism. As with Justin, initiation was subsequent to repentance of sin. When the initiate came to the rite itself, he or she was plunged into the water. The physical act of immersion resulted in the spiritual effect of freedom from sins.

Chapter Two

How great is the force of perversity for so shaking the faith or entirely preventing its reception, that it impugns it on the very principles of which the faith consists! There is absolutely nothing which makes men's minds more obdurate than the simplicity of the divine works which are visible in the act of baptism, when they are compared with the promise in the effect. The consequent attainment of eternity is esteemed the more incredible because it is with so great simplicity, without pomp, without any considerable novelty of preparation, finally, without expense, that a person is dipped in water, and amid the utterance of some few words is sprinkled and then rises again, not much (or not at all) the cleaner.

Chapter Seven

After this, when we have issued from the baptismal pool, we are thoroughly anointed with a blessed unction, a practice derived from the old discipline, wherein on entering the priesthood, men were anointed with oil from a horn, ever since Aaron was anointed by Moses. From this Aaron is called "Christ," from the "chrism," which is the "unction." When understood spiritually this furnishes an appropriate name to the Lord, because he was "anointed" with the Spirit by God the Father, as written in the book of Acts, "For truly they were gathered together in this city against your Holy Son whom you have anointed." Thus too, in our case, the unction runs carnally (i.e. on the body) but profits spiritually; in the same way as the act of baptism itself is also carnal, in that we are plunged into water, but the effect spiritual, in that we are freed from sins.

Chapter Eight

In the next place is the laying on of hands, invoking and inviting the Holy Spirit through benediction. Shall it be granted possible for human ingenuity to summon a spirit into water, and by the application of hands from above to animate their union into one body with another spirit of so clear sound? Shall it not be possible for God, in the case of his own organ, to produce by means of "holy hands" a sublime spiritual modulation? But this, as well as the former, is derived from the old sacramental rite in which Jacob blessed his grandsons, born of Joseph, Ephraim, and Manasseh; with his hands laid on them and interchanged, and indeed so transversely slanted one over the other, that by delineating Christ they even foreshadowed the future benediction into Christ.

Chapter Eighteen

But they whose office it is know that baptism is not to be administered hastily. "Give to every one who asks you," has a reference of its own, pertaining especially to giving alms. Conversely, one should consider carefully these instructions: "Give not the holy thing to the dogs, nor cast your pearls before swine"; and, "Do not lay hands hastily on anyone; share not in their sins." . . . Therefore, according to the circumstances, disposition, and even age of each individual, the delay of baptism is preferable, especially in the case of little children. Why is it necessary that the sponsors should be thrust into danger if baptism itself is not necessary for salvation? They, by reason of mortality, may fail to fulfill their promises as sponsors, and may also be disappointed by the development of an evil disposition in those whom they sponsored? The Lord does indeed say, "Do not forbid them to come to me." Let them come while they are growing up. Let them come while they are learning where they are coming. Let them become Christians when they are able to know Christ. Why does the innocent period of life hasten to the "remission of sins"? More caution is exercised in worldly matters, in that the one who is not trusted with earthly substance is entrusted with divine! Let them know how to ask for salvation, that you may be seen to have given "to the one who asks." For no less cause must the unmarried also be deferred, in whom the ground of temptation is prepared, until they either marry, or else be more fully strengthened for continence. This includes both those who were never married, by means of their maturity, and those widowed, by means of their freedom. If any understand the weighty importance of baptism, they will fear its reception more than its delay: sound faith is secure of salvation.

Chapter Nineteen

The Passover affords a more than usually solemn day for baptism because this was when the Lord's passion, into which we are baptized, was completed. Nor will it be incongruous to interpret figuratively the fact that, when the Lord was about to celebrate the last Passover, he said to the disciples who were sent to make preparation, "You will meet a man bearing water." He points out the place for celebrating the Passover by the sign of water.

After that, Pentecost is a most joyous occasion for conferring baptisms because then the resurrection of the Lord was repeatedly proven among the disciples, and the hope of the advent of the Lord indirectly pointed to, in that, at that time, when he had been received back into the heavens, the angels told the apostles that "He would so come, as he had ascended into the heavens"; at Pentecost, of course. But, moreover, when Jeremiah says, "And I will gather them together from the extremities of the land in the feast-day," he signifies the day of the Passover and of Pentecost, which is properly a "feast-day." However, every day is the Lord's; every hour, every time, is apt for baptism. Although there is a difference in the solemnity, there is no distinction in the grace.

Chapter Twenty

They who are about to enter baptism ought to pray with repeated prayers, fasts, and bending of the knee. There should be vigils all through the night accompanied by the confession of all past sins, that they may express the meaning even of the baptism of John: "They were baptized," says the Scripture, "confessing their own sins." To us it is matter for thankfulness if we do now publicly confess our iniquities or our turpitudes: for we do at the same time both make satisfaction for our former sins, by mortification of our flesh and spirit, and lay beforehand the foundation of defenses against the temptations which will closely follow. "Watch and pray," says the Lord, "lest you fall into temptation." And the reason, I believe, why they were tempted was that they fell asleep. The result was that they deserted the Lord when apprehended, and he who continued to stand by him, and used the sword, even denied him three times. The word had gone before that "no one who has not been tempted should attain the celestial kingdoms." The Lord himself was surrounded by temptations after his baptism, when in forty days he had fasted. "Then," someone will say, "we also should fast after baptism." Well, and who forbids you, unless it be the necessity for joy, and the thanksgiving for salvation? But so far as I, with my poor powers, understand, the Lord figuratively retorted upon Israel the reproach they had cast on the Lord. For the people, after crossing the sea, and being carried about in the desert during forty years, although they were there nourished with divine supplies, nevertheless were more mindful of their belly and their gullet than of God. Thereupon the Lord, driven apart into desert places after his baptism, by means of a forty-day fast, showed that the man of God lives "not by bread alone," but "by the word of God." He also showed that temptations incident to fullness or immoderation of appetite are shattered by abstinence.

ANF 3, ed. A. Cleveland Coxe. Reprint, Peabody, MA: Hendrickson, 1994.

Cyprian of Carthage (200–258)

Letter 58

Cyprian was bishop of the North African city of Carthage in the immediate aftermath of the disastrous persecution by Emperor Decius. In 250 the emperor had required all inhabitants of the empire to offer sacrifice to the god Jupiter. Upon making the offering one would have received a certificate, called a *libellus,* confirming that the rite had been performed. Christians considered such an act to be treason, though many of them did sacrifice.

The Christian community struggled with how to handle the large number of its members who had capitulated under pressure and sacrificed to false gods. One party, called the Novatianists after their leader Novatian, wished to offer the "lapsed," or fallen, no chance of forgiveness and return to the community. Another party, the Catholics, offered unconditional acceptance back into favorable standing with the church. Cyprian addressed this issue by taking a somewhat middle ground, offering readmittance to those willing to perform penance. He also required the rebaptism of Novatianists who wished to convert.

This letter was intended to address the question of baptizing infants. In it, Cyprian announced the decision of an African synod in 253 approving of infant baptism. One significant element of Cyprian's own understanding of baptism is that it was not only appropriate for infants but also useful because it offers them the mercy and grace of God. He argued that one should not equate baptism with circumcision, which other writers, including Augustine, were so quick to do.

Another important aspect of his instruction was his reason for baptizing infants: the sacrament conferred the mercy and grace of God upon the recipient. Here one finds a greater emphasis on the importance of the act to the individual. With a greater emphasis on the effect of baptism on the one being baptized, the corporate nature of the ceremony is diminished. Baptism becomes less a rite of initiation into a like-minded community and more a means to personal salvation.

2. But in respect of the case of the infants, which you say ought not to be baptized within the second or third day after their birth, and that the law of ancient circumcision should be regarded, so that you think that one who is just

born should not be baptized and sanctified within the eighth day, we all thought very differently in our council. For in this course which you thought was to be taken, no one agreed; but we all rather judge that the mercy and grace of God is not to be refused to any one born of man. For as the Lord says in his gospel, "The Son of man is not come to destroy men's lives, but to save them," as far as we can, we must strive that, if possible, no soul be lost. For what is wanting to him who has once been formed in the womb by the hand of God? . . . Whatever things are made by God, are completed by the majesty and work of God their Maker. . . .

6. And therefore, dearest brother, this was our opinion in council, that by us no one ought to be hindered from baptism and from the grace of God, who is merciful and kind and loving to all. Which, since it is to be observed and maintained in respect of all, we think it to be even more observed in respect of infants and newly-born persons, who on this very account deserve more from our help and from the divine mercy, that immediately, on the very beginning of their birth, lamenting and weeping, they do nothing else but entreat.

ANF 5, ed. A. Cleveland Coxe. Reprint, Peabody, MA: Hendrickson, 1994.

Apostolic Constitutions (Fourth Century)

Written near the end of the fourth century, this work is essentially a compilation of portions of earlier church orders, including the *Didache,* the *Didascalia Apostolorum,* and Hippolytus' *Apostolic Traditions.* As such, it affords the reader a glimpse into liturgical tradition, as well as church practice in the fourth century, making it an important collection.

A few commonalities between this selection and the selections we have seen thus far are obvious. An explicit reference to Jesus' instruction to his disciples provided the basis for baptism,[6] the initiate was to prepare by fasting, and the one administering the sacrament was to do so in the name of the Father, the Son, and the Holy Spirit, the typical Triune formula. A significant emphasis in this document is that baptism is a type, or symbol, of the believer's sharing in the death of Christ. Christians are those who have died and been resurrected with him. His own baptism served as the example for Christian baptism. Immersion into the water symbolized burial into the ground. Other symbolism was the anointing with oil, which was to be done twice. The first time it illustrated the Holy Spirit coming to dwell within the convert. The second time it was a seal of the covenant between God and the believer.

The *Constitutions* allowed for baptism to be performed only by a bishop or a presbyter.[7] Deacons and deaconesses assisted the minister by helping those who had been baptized out of the baptismal pool and anointing them with oil as a symbol of their commitment to the community. The initiates would have been naked during their baptism, so deacons would receive the men and deaconesses the women in order to preserve decency.

Book Three, Section Two

16. You, O bishop, shall anoint the head of those that are to be baptized, whether they be men or women, with the holy oil, for a symbol of the spiritual baptism. After that, either you or a presbyter that is under you, shall in the solemn form name over them the Father, and Son, and Holy Spirit, and shall immerse them in the water. Let a deacon receive the man, and a deaconess the woman, that so the conferring of this inviolable seal may take place with appropriate decency. And after that, let the bishop anoint those that are baptized with ointment.

17. This baptism, therefore, is given into the death of Jesus. There is water instead of the burial, oil instead of the Holy Spirit, and the seal instead of the cross. The ointment is the confirmation of the confession. The Father is named because he is the Author and Sender. The Holy Spirit is jointly named because he is the witness. The descent into the water represents the dying together with Christ, and the ascent out of the water the rising again with him. The Father is the God over all; Christ is the Only-begotten God, the beloved Son, the Lord of glory; the Holy Spirit is the Comforter, who is sent by Christ, taught by him, and proclaims him.

Book Seven, Section Two

22. Now concerning baptism, bishop or presbyter, we have already given direction, and we now say, that you should so baptize as the Lord commanded us, saying, "Go and teach all nations, baptizing them in the name of the Father, and of the Son, and of the Holy Spirit teaching them to observe all things whatsoever I have commanded you." Baptize in the name of the Fa-

ther who sent, of Christ who came, of the Comforter who testified. But you should beforehand anoint the person with the holy oil, and afterward baptize him with the water, and in the conclusion shall seal him with the ointment. The anointing with oil is the participation of the Holy Spirit, and the water the symbol of the death of Christ, and the ointment the seal of the covenants. But if there is neither oil nor ointment, water is sufficient both for the anointing, and for the seal, and for the confession of him that is dead, or indeed is dying together with Christ. But before baptism, let him that is to be baptized fast; for even the Lord, when he was first baptized by John, and abode in the wilderness, did afterward fast forty days and forty nights. But he was baptized, and then fasted, not having himself any need of cleansing, or of fasting, or of purgation, who was by nature pure and holy; but that he might testify the truth to John, and afford an example to us. Our Lord was not baptized into his own passion, or death, or resurrection—for none of those things had then happened—but for another purpose. Therefore he by his own authority fasted after his baptism, as being the Lord of John. But he who is to be initiated into his death ought first to fast, and then to be baptized. For it is not reasonable that he who has been buried with Christ, and is risen again with him, should appear dejected at his very resurrection. For man is not Lord of our Savior's constitution, since one is the Master and the other the servant.

Book Seven, Section Three

41. "I renounce Satan, and his works, and his pomp, and his worships, and his angels, and his inventions, and all things that are under him." And after this renunciation let him in his consociation say, "And I associate myself to Christ, and believe, and am baptized into one unbegotten Being, the only true God Almighty, the Father of Christ, the Creator and Maker of all things, from whom are all things; and into the Lord Jesus Christ, his Only-begotten Son, the first-born of the whole creation, who before the ages was begotten by the good pleasure of the Father, by whom all things were made, both those in heaven and those on earth, visible and invisible. Who in the last days descended from heaven, took flesh, was born of the holy Virgin Mary, did converse in a holy manner according to the laws of his God and Father, was crucified under Pontius Pilate, died for us, rose again from the dead the third day after his passion, ascended

into the heavens, sits at the right hand of the Father, and again is to come at the end of the world with glory to judge the living and the dead, of whose kingdom there shall be no end. And I am baptized into the Holy Spirit, that is, the Comforter, who worked in all the saints from the beginning of the world, but was afterwards sent to the apostles by the Father, according to the promise of our Savior and Lord, Jesus Christ. After the apostles, was sent to all those that believe in the Holy Universal Church; into the resurrection of the flesh, and into the remission of sins, and into the kingdom of heaven, and into the life of the world to come." And after this vow, he comes in order to the anointing with oil. . . .

43. After this he comes to the water, and blesses and glorifies the Lord God Almighty, the Father of the Only-begotten God. The minister returns thanks that he has sent his Son to become human on our account, that he might save us; that he has permitted that he should in all things become obedient to the laws of that incarnation, to preach the kingdom of heaven, the remission of sins, and the resurrection of the dead. Moreover, he adores the Only-begotten God himself, after his Father, and for him, giving him thanks that he undertook to die for all humanity by the cross, the type of which he has appointed to be the baptism of regeneration. He glorifies him also, for that God who is the Lord of the whole world, in the name of Christ and by his Holy Spirit, has not cast off humanity but has suited his providence to the difference of seasons. At first he gave to Adam himself paradise for a habitation of pleasure, and afterwards he gave a command on account of providence, and rightly cast out the offender. However, through his goodness he did not completely cast him off, but instructed his posterity in succeeding ages after various manners; on whose account, in the conclusion of the world, he has sent his Son to become human for humanity's sake, and to undergo all human passions without sin. That person, therefore, let the minister even now call upon in baptism, and let him say, "Look down from heaven, and sanctify this water, and give it grace and power, that so he that is to be baptized, according to the command of your Christ, may be crucified with him, and may die with him, and may be buried with him, and may rise with him to the adoption which is in him, that he may be dead to sin and live to righteousness." And after this, when he has baptized him in the name of the Father, and of the Son, and of the Holy Spirit, he shall anoint him with ointment.

ANF 7, ed. A. Cleveland Coxe. Reprint, Peabody, MA: Hendrickson, 1994.

Hilary of Poitiers (315–367)

On the Trinity

Hilary became bishop of Poitiers in Gaul around 353. In 356, he was exiled by the emperor for refusing to condemn Athanasius of Alexandria. Behind this event lay the complex Arian controversy in which the teachings of Arius of Alexandria had been denounced at the First Ecumenical Council of Nicaea in 325. Emperor Constantine had called the gathering to encourage Christians to settle the question of the deity of Christ as the Son of God. The council produced the historic Nicene Creed, which is still used today in a version revised at the Second Ecumenical Council of Constantinople in 381. Immediately following the decision by the leaders at Nicaea, pastors of the Arian persuasion were exiled. Soon, however, they were recalled and the anti-Arian orthodox, including Athanasius, were removed from office. Hilary's refusal to support this imperial action led to his own exile to Phrygia.

Hilary's time out of office afforded him the opportunity to become well acquainted with the important Greek theologians who had defended the theology of Nicaea. He became one of the most important anti-Arian theologians in the West. This particular treatise, *On the Trinity*, was composed between 356 and 360, and was intended to be a refutation of Arianism as well as a description of orthodox theology concerning the Trinity.

This selection shows Hilary's insistence that Trinitarian theology and baptismal practice were inextricably linked. He derived his understanding of baptism from the instruction Christ gave to the disciples just before his ascension. He claims that in this passage one finds (1) the Triune formula that is to be used (exhibiting, for Hilary, a picture of the Trinity), (2) the acts to be performed, (3) the order of the process, and (4) insight into the nature of the Trinity.

Book Two, Chapter One

Believers have always found their satisfaction in that Divine utterance, which our ears heard recited from the Gospel at the moment when that Power, which is its attestation, was bestowed upon us: "Go now and teach all nations, baptizing them in the Name of the Father, and of the Son, and of the Holy Spirit, teaching them to observe all things whatsoever I command you;

and, behold, I am with you always, even unto the end of the world." What element in the mystery of humanity's salvation is not included in those words? What is forgotten, what left in darkness? All is full, as from the Divine fullness. All is perfect, as from the Divine perfection. The passage contains the exact words to be used, the essential acts, the sequence of processes, and insight into the Divine nature. He instructed them to baptize in the Name of the Father, and of the Son, and of the Holy Spirit; that is, with confession of the Creator, of the Only-begotten, and of the Gift. For God the Father is one, from whom are all things. Our Lord Jesus Christ the Only-begotten is one, through whom are all things. The Spirit, God's Gift to us is also one, who pervades all things. Thus all are arranged according to powers possessed and benefits conferred: the one Power from whom all things, the one Offspring through whom all things, the one Gift who gives us perfect hope. Nothing can be found lacking in that supreme union which embraces infinity in the eternal (in "Father"), his likeness in his express image (in "Son"), and our enjoyment of him in the Gift (in "Holy Spirit").

NPNF 2.9, ed. W. Sanday. Reprint, Peabody, MA: Hendrickson, 1994.

Gregory of Nazianzus (329–390)
Oration 40: On Baptism

Gregory is one of the more important theologians in Christian history. As Bishop of Constantinople, he presided over the Council of Constantinople in 381. He is known for his twofold polemic against Apollinarius of Alexandria and Eunomius. The former theologian denied the existence of a human mind in Christ, thus disallowing his complete humanity, a teaching that was condemned at the Second Ecumenical Council. Eunomius was an ardent proponent of Arianism. In addition, Gregory is remembered for his excellence as a pastor and preacher, which is demonstrated in the significant *Orations,* as well as his many hymns. He is one of the so-called Cappadocian Fathers along with Basil (the Great) of Caesarea and Gregory of Nyssa. The Cappadocians, a term taken from the area of Cappadocia, where they were from, together defended Nicene theology against both Arianism and Apollinarianism.

This oration was preached on the occasion of the Feast of the Lights, in commemoration of Christ's own baptism and the example it provided the church. Gregory spoke of the rite of baptism being known by several different names, each of which represented some component of the sacrament. For example, he called it the bath of regeneration because the baptized was washed clean of sin. It was called baptism because the sinner was buried in the water.

Gregory instructed that infant baptism should be performed only when there was a present danger to the life of the child. The act was beneficial to the child even though the child could not yet exercise his or her rational faculties, just as circumcision was of benefit to the children of Israel who received it. However, his advice was to delay baptism until at least after the third year, in order that the child may understand at least something of the sacrament. Here one finds not only the growing emphasis on the effects of baptism on the recipient but a continuation of the importance for initiation into the community.

Central in these selections was Gregory's justification for the importance of baptism. He proposed that because human beings are made of a visible body and an invisible soul, there must be both a visible and an invisible cleansing. The visible cleansing was that of the water, and it was a symbol of the inner, invisible cleansing by the Spirit.

2. The Word recognizes three births for us; namely, the natural birth, that of baptism, and that of the resurrection.

3. Concerning two of these births, the first and the last, we have not to speak on the present occasion. Let us discourse upon the second, which is now necessary for us, and which gives its name to the Feast of the Lights. Illumination is the splendor of souls, the conversion of the life, the question put to the God-ward conscience. It is the aid to our weakness, the renunciation of the flesh, the following of the Spirit, the fellowship of the Word, the improvement of the creature, the overwhelming of sin, the participation of light, the dissolution of darkness. It is the carriage to God, the dying with Christ, the perfecting of the mind, the bulwark of Faith, the key of the Kingdom of heaven, the change of life, the removal of slavery, the loosing of chains, the remodeling of the whole man. Why should I go into further detail? Illumination is the greatest and most magnificent of the Gifts of God. For just as we speak of the Holy of Holies, and the Song of Songs, as more comprehensive and more excellent than others, so is this called Illumination, as being more holy than any other illumination which we possess.

4. And as Christ the Giver of it is called by many various names, so too is

this Gift, whether it is from the exceeding gladness of its nature (as those who are very fond of a thing take pleasure in using its name), or that the great variety of its benefits has reacted for us upon its names. We call it, the Gift, the Grace, baptism, Unction, Illumination, the Clothing of Immortality, the Bath of Regeneration, the Seal, and everything that is honorable. We call it the Gift, because it is given to us in return for nothing on our part; Grace, because it is conferred even on debtors; baptism, because sin is buried with it in the water; Unction, as Priestly and Royal, for such were they who were anointed; Illumination, because of its splendor; Clothing, because it hides our shame; the Bath, because it washes us; the Seal because it preserves us, and is moreover the indication of Dominion. In it the heavens rejoice; it is glorified by angels, because of its kindred splendor. It is the image of the heavenly bliss. We long indeed to sing out its praises, but we cannot worthily do so. . . .

8. And since we are double-made, I mean of body and soul, and the one part is visible, the other invisible, so the cleansing also is twofold, by water and the spirit; the one received visibly in the body, the other concurring with it invisibly and apart from the body; the one typical, the other real and cleansing the depths. And this which comes to the aid of our first birth, makes us new instead of old, and like God instead of what we now are; recasting us without fire, and creating us anew without breaking us up, For, to say it all in one word, the virtue of baptism is to be understood as a covenant with God for a second life and a purer conversation. . . .

28. Be it so, some will say, in the case of those who ask for baptism; what have you to say about those who are still children, and conscious neither of the loss nor of the grace? Are we to baptize them too? Certainly, if any danger presses. For it is better that they should be unconsciously sanctified than that they should depart unsealed and uninitiated. A proof of this is found in the circumcision on the eighth day, which was a sort of typical seal, and was conferred on children before they had the use of reason. And so is the anointing of the doorposts, which preserved the firstborn, though applied to things which had no consciousness. But in respect of others I give my advice to wait till the end of the third year, or a little more or less, when they may be able to listen and to answer something about the sacrament; that, even though they do not perfectly understand it, yet at any rate they may know the outlines; and then to sanctify them in soul and body with the great sacrament of our consecration. For this is how the matter stands; at that time they begin to be responsible for their lives, when reason is matured, and they learn the

mystery of life—for of sins of ignorance owing to their tender years they have no account to give—and it is far more profitable on all accounts to be fortified by the font, because of the sudden assaults of danger that befall us, stronger than our helpers.

NPNF 2.7, ed. W. Sanday. Reprint, Peabody, MA: Hendrickson, 1994.

Cyril of Jerusalem (315–386)
Catechetical Lecture 19

Cyril's catechetical lectures, probably delivered in the Lenten season of the year he became Bishop of Jerusalem (350), cover a wide diversity of fundamental aspects of Christian faith and practice. Though he spent some twelve years in exile on three different occasions for his anti-Arian position and for a questionable sale of church artifacts, Cyril was able to have a significant influence on the church, primarily through his lectures.

This selection is from the first of two messages delivered on consecutive days to catechumens in preparation for their baptism. Cyril described for them events that occurred in the vestibule area, before actually entering the inner chamber of the baptismal pool itself.

The acts that took place in the outer chamber focused on the renunciation of Satan, his works, and his ways. The catechumen faced west for the renunciation because the West symbolized the region of darkness. In renouncing Satan and his ways, the initiate pledged to abandon the former manner of living and to now live in obedience to Christ. The emphasis in this lecture is the individual's personal commitment to Christ.

2. First you enter into the vestibule of the baptistery, and there facing towards the West you listen to the command to stretch forth your hand, and as if in the presence of Satan you renounce him. Now you must know that this figure is found in ancient history. For when Pharaoh, that most bitter and cruel tyrant, was oppressing the free and high-born people of the Hebrews, God sent Moses to bring them out of the evil bondage of the Egyptians. Then the door posts were anointed with the blood of a lamb, that the destroyer might flee from the houses which had the sign of the blood; and the Hebrew people was marvelously delivered. The enemy, however, after their rescue, "pursued after them," and saw the sea wondrously parted for them; nevertheless

he went on, following close in their footsteps, and was all at once over-whelmed and engulfed in the Red Sea. . . .

4. But nevertheless you are instructed to say, with arms outstretched to-wards him as though he were present, "I renounce you, Satan." I wish also to say why you stand facing to the West, because it is necessary. Since the West is the region of sensible darkness, and he being darkness has his dominion also in darkness, therefore, looking with a symbolical meaning towards the West, you renounce that dark and gloomy potentate. What then did each of you stand up and say? "I renounce you, Satan, you wicked and most cruel tyrant!" meaning, "I fear your might no longer; for Christ has overthrown you, having partaken with me of flesh and blood, that through these he 'might by death destroy death,' that I might not be made 'subject to bondage' forever. I renounce you, you crafty and most subtle serpent. I renounce you, plotter as you are, who under the guise of friendship did contrive all disobe-dience, and worked apostasy in our first parents. I renounce you, Satan, the artificer and abettor of all wickedness."

5. Then in a second sentence you are taught to say, "and all your works." Now the works of Satan are all sin, which also you must renounce; just as one who has escaped a tyrant has surely escaped his weapons also. All sin there-fore, of every kind, is included in the works of the devil. Only know this; that all that you say, especially at that most thrilling hour, is written in God's books. Therefore, when you do anything contrary to these promises, you shall be judged as "a transgressor." You renounce therefore the works of Satan; I mean, all deeds and thoughts which are contrary to reason.

6. Then you say, "And all his pomp." Now the pomp of the devil is the madness of theatres, and horse-races, and hunting, and all such vanity, from which that holy man praying to be delivered says unto God, "Turn away mine eyes from beholding vanity." Do not be interested in the madness of the theater, where you will behold the wanton gestures of the players, carried on with mockeries and all unseemliness, and the frantic dancing of effeminate men. Neither be interested in the madness of those who in hunts expose themselves to wild beasts, that they may pamper their miserable appetite; who, to serve their belly with meats, become themselves in reality meat for the belly of untamed beasts. To speak justly, they cast away their life head-long in single combats for the sake of their own god, i.e. their belly. Shun also horse-racing, that frantic and soul-subverting spectacle; For all these are the pomp of the devil. . . .

11. And these things were done in the outer chamber. But if God wills, when in the succeeding lectures on the Mysteries we have entered into the Holy of Holies, we shall there know the symbolical meaning of the things which are there performed. Now to God the Father, with the Son and the Holy Spirit, be glory, and power, and majesty, forever and ever. Amen.

NPNF 2.7, ed. W. Sanday. Reprint, Peabody, MA: Hendrickson, 1994.

Cyril of Jerusalem (315–386)

Catechetical Lecture 20

In this second lecture from a series dedicated to explaining the baptism ceremony to catechumens, Cyril indicated that once in the inner chamber those being baptized would disrobe as a symbol of putting off the former way of life. In being naked, the initiate imitated Christ, who hung on the cross naked. An anointing would be next, which symbolized grafting into Christ. Then, the catechumen would be taken to the pool and asked to make the Triune confession of belief in the Father, the Son, and the Holy Spirit. He or she would then be dipped three times under the water, representing the three days Christ was in the grave. Rising from the water would have indicated a new birth for the believer. Once again, the emphasis is on the individual rather than the community, without negating the importance of baptism as a rite of initiation.

1. These daily introductions into the Mysteries, and new instructions, which are the announcements of new truths, are profitable to us; and most of all to you, who have been renewed from an old state to a new. Therefore, I shall necessarily lay before you the sequel of yesterday's lecture, that you may learn what those things which were done by you in the inner chamber symbolized.

2. As soon as you entered the chamber you put off your tunic, which was an image of "putting off the old man with his deeds." Having stripped yourselves, you were naked. In this also you were imitating Christ, who was stripped naked on the cross, and by his nakedness "put off from himself the principalities and powers, and openly triumphed over them on the tree." For since the adverse powers made their lair in your members, you may no longer

wear that old garment. I do not at all mean this visible one, but "the old man, which waxes corrupt in the lusts of deceit." May the soul which has once put him off, never again put him on, but say with the Bride of Christ in the Song of Songs, "I have put off my garment, how shall I put it on?" O wondrous thing, you were naked in the sight of all, and were not ashamed; for truly you bore the likeness of the first-formed Adam, who was naked in the garden, and was not ashamed.

3. Then, when you were stripped, you were anointed with exorcised oil, from the very hairs of your head to your feet, and were made partakers of the good olive-tree, Jesus Christ. For you were cut off from the wild olive-tree, and grafted into the good one, and were made to share the fatness of the true olive-tree. The exorcised oil therefore was a symbol of the participation of the fatness of Christ, being a charm to drive away every trace of hostile influence. For as the breathing of the saints, and the invocation of the Name of God, like fiercest flame, scorch and drive out evil spirits, so also this exorcised oil receives such virtue by the invocation of God and by prayer, as not only to burn and cleanse away the traces of sins, but also to chase away all the invisible powers of the evil one.

4. After these things, you were led to the holy pool of Divine baptism, as Christ was carried from the cross to the sepulcher which is before our eyes. Then each of you was asked whether he believed in the name of the Father, and of the Son, and of the Holy Spirit. Then you made that saving confession, and descended three times into the water, and ascended again; here also showing by a symbol the three days burial of Christ. For as our Savior passed three days and three nights in the heart of the earth, so you also in your first ascent out of the water, represented the first day of Christ in the earth, and by your descent, the night; for as he who is in the night, no longer sees, but he who is in the day, remains in the light, so in the descent, as in the night, you saw nothing, but in ascending again you were as in the day. And at the very same moment you were both dying and being born. That water of salvation was at once your grave and your mother. And what Solomon spoke of others will suit you also; for he said, in that case, "There is a time to bear and a time to die." This was in the reverse order for you: there was a time to die and a time to be born. Moreover, one and the same time effected both of these, and your birth went hand in hand with your death.

NPNF 2.7, ed. W. Sanday. Reprint, Peabody, MA: Hendrickson, 1994.

Ambrose of Milan (339–397)

On the Mysteries

Ambrose is esteemed as one of the "Doctors" [important teachers] of the Western church, indicating his immense influence on its faith and practice. He was Bishop of Milan from 374 to 397 after having served as a governor in northern Italy from 370. He is often referred to as the Father of Liturgical Hymnody, because of the numerous hymns he produced. Ambrose is also known for his most famous convert, Augustine of Hippo. This particular treatise offers a glimpse into the understanding and practice of the sacraments in the Western church of the fourth century.

Ambrose described the purpose of baptism as the washing away or remission of sins. In fact, he claimed that even if the catechumen believed in the cross of Christ, unless he was baptized he would not receive the remission of sins. The cleansing that baptism effected was symbolized by the participant's wearing a white robe after being baptized. This washing took place not because of the water but because of the presence of God in the event. Without the Spirit of God present in the baptism, there would be no remission of sins. For Ambrose, the proper mode of baptism was immersion, which he spoke of as a dipping of the participant, symbolizing one's burial. This "death to sin" and cleansing of sin took place when the initiate went down into the water and was immersed in it. The effect of the rite on the individual was foremost for Ambrose.

It was necessary that the Triune formula be used for the baptism to be valid because this had been commanded by Christ. The candidate would be asked whether or not he or she confessed the Father, the Son, and the Holy Spirit, and upon that confession would be baptized in the name of the Trinity.

Chapter Three

8. What did you see? Water, certainly, but not water alone; you saw the deacons ministering there, and the bishop asking questions and consecrating. First of all, the Apostle taught you that those things are not to be considered "which we see, but the things which are not seen, for the things which are seen are temporal, but the things which are not seen are eternal." For you read elsewhere: "That the invisible things of God, since the creation of the

world, are understood through those things which have been made; his eternal power also and Godhead are estimated by his works." Wherefore also the Lord himself says, "If you do not believe me, at least believe my works." Believe, then, that the presence of the Godhead is there. Do you believe the working, and not believe the presence? Whence should the working proceed unless the presence went before? . . .

10. All flesh was corrupt by its iniquities. "My Spirit," says God, "shall not remain among men, because they are flesh." Whereby God shows that the grace of the Spirit is turned away by carnal impurity and the pollution of grave sin. Upon which God, willing to restore what was lacking, sent the flood and bade just Noah go up into the ark. And he, after having, as the flood was passing off, sent forth first a raven which did not return, sent forth a dove which is said to have returned with an olive twig. You see the water, you see the wood of the ark, you see the dove, and do you hesitate as to the mystery?

11. The water, then, is that in which the flesh is dipped, that all carnal sin may be washed away. All wickedness is there buried. The wood is that on which the Lord Jesus was fastened when he suffered for us. The dove is that in the form of which the Holy Spirit descended, as you have read in the New Testament, Who inspires in you peace of soul and tranquility of mind. The raven is the figure of sin, which goes forth and does not return, if, in you, too, inwardly and outwardly righteousness be preserved.

Chapter Four

19. The reason why you were told before not to believe only what you saw was that you might not say perchance, "This is that great mystery 'which eye hath not seen, nor ear heard, neither has it entered into the heart of man.' I see water, which I have been used to seeing every day. Is that water to cleanse me now in which I have so often bathed without ever being cleansed?" By this you may recognize that water does not cleanse without the Spirit.

20. Therefore read that the three witnesses in baptism, the water, the blood, and the Spirit are one, for if you take away one of these, the Sacrament of baptism does not exist. For what is water without the cross of Christ? It is merely a common element, without any sacramental effect. Nor, again, is there the Sacrament of Regeneration without water: "For except a man be born again of water and of the Spirit, he cannot enter into the kingdom of

God." Now, even the catechumen believes in the cross of the Lord Jesus, wherewith he too is signed; but unless he be baptized in the Name of the Father, and of the Son, and of the Holy Spirit, he cannot receive remission of sins nor gain the gift of spiritual grace.

21. So that Syrian dipped himself seven times under the law, but you were baptized in the Name of the Trinity, you confessed the Father. Call to mind what you did: you confessed the Son, you confessed the Holy Spirit. Mark well the order of things in this faith: you died to the world, and rose again to God. And as though buried to the world in that element, being dead to sin, you rose again to eternal life. Believe, therefore, that these waters are not void of power.

Chapter Five

28. Remember when you went down into the water how you replied to the questions, that you believe in the Father, that you believe in the Son, that you believe in the Holy Spirit. The statement there is not: I believe in a greater and in a less and in a lowest person, but you are bound by the same guarantee of your own voice, to believe in the Son in like manner as you believe in the Father; and to believe in the Holy Spirit in like manner as you believe in the Son, with this one exception, that you confess that you must believe in the cross of the Lord Jesus alone.

Chapter Seven

34. After this white robes were given to you as a sign that you were putting off the covering of sins, and putting on the chaste veil of innocence, of which the prophet said, "You shall sprinkle me with hyssop and I shall be cleansed, you shall wash me and I shall be made whiter than snow." For he who is baptized is seen to be purified both according to the Law and according to the Gospel: according to the Law, because Moses sprinkled the blood of the lamb with a bunch of hyssop; according to the Gospel, because Christ's garments were white as snow, when in the Gospel he showed forth the glory of his resurrection. Therefore, he whose guilt is remitted is made whiter than snow. So that God said by Isaiah: "Though your sins be as scarlet, I will make them white as snow."

NPNF 2.10, ed. W. Sanday. Reprint, Peabody, MA: Hendrickson, 1994.

John Chrysostom of Constantinople (347–407)

First Instruction to Catechumens

In 398, John was appointed Bishop of Constantinople. Though his ministry began calmly, he soon became entangled in controversy, with both Theophilus Bishop of Alexandria and the Empress Eudoxia. In 403, a group of monks (the "Tall Brothers") who had been accused of heresy and insubordination to the bishop in Alexandria fled to Constantinople. John refused to condemn them without a trial. Added to this was John's incessant preaching against luxurious living in the imperial city and a reference to "Jezebel" in one of his sermons, which was taken as a jab at the empress. Theophilus called a synod at the Oak, near Chalcedon, and John was deposed by mainly Egyptian bishops. However, he was recalled to his bishopric only soon to be exiled because of continuing controversy with Eudoxia.

Despite dying in exile, John's influence in the church remained strong. The Bishop of Rome continued to support him while in exile, and his name was soon returned to the diptychs, or list of significant bishops. Though not revered as a theologian per se, John was revered for his preaching; thus the appellation "Chrysostom," or "Golden-tongued." His sermons on numerous books of the Bible are a tribute to his ministry. These selections from a message to catechumens and a sermon on Ephesians are representative of the many homilies he preached while in Constantinople.

Here we find Chrysostom's instructions to the catechumens about the sacrament of baptism, addressing such concerns as the title for the rite, the reason for performing it, and the results from it. He spoke of the cleansing that comes from the "bath of regeneration," which he contrasted with pagan baths and Jewish baptism. The latter two, he contended, were not intended to cleanse the individual participant of sin. As he taught those preparing for initiation into the community, John's most important concern was the common experience shared by all its members: cleansing from sin.

2. The one who is about to approach these holy and dread mysteries must be awake and alert, must be clean from all cares of this life, full of much self-restraint and readiness. He must banish from his mind every thought foreign to the mysteries, and on all sides cleanse and prepare his home, as if about to receive the king himself. Such is the preparation of your mind, such are your

thoughts, such the purpose of your soul. Await therefore a return worthy of this most excellent decision from God, who overpowers with His recompense those who show forth obedience to him. . . . I wished to say this first of all, why in the world our fathers, passing by the whole year, settled that the children of the Church should be initiated at this season. And for what reason, after the instruction from us, removing your shoes and raiment, unclad and unshod, with but one garment on, they conduct you to hear the words of those exorcising. For it is not thoughtlessly and rashly that they have planned this dress and this season for us. But both these things have a certain mystic and secret reason. And I wished to say this to you. But I see that our discourse now constrains us to something more necessary. For it is necessary to say what baptism is, and for what reason it enters into our life, and what good things it conveys to us.

But, if you will, let us discourse about the name which this mystic cleansing bears: for its name is not one, but very many and various. For this purification is called the bath of regeneration. "He saved us," he says, "through the bath of regeneration, and renewing of the Holy Spirit." It is called also illumination as Paul has called it, "For call to remembrance the former days in which after you were illuminated you endured a great conflict of sufferings"; and again, "For it is impossible for those who were once illuminated, and have tasted of the heavenly gift, and then fell away, to renew themselves again unto repentance." It is also called baptism: "For as many of you as were baptized into Christ did put on Christ." It is also called burial: "For we were buried" he says, "with him, through baptism, into death." It is called circumcision: "In whom you were also circumcised, with a circumcision not made with hands, in the putting off of the body of the sins of the flesh." It is called a cross: "Our old man was crucified with him that the body of sin might be done away." . . . There is that bath by means of the baths, common to all men, which is to wipe off bodily uncleanness. Then there is the Jewish bath, more honorable than the other, but far inferior to that of grace. It too wipes off bodily uncleanness, but not simply uncleanness of body, since it even reaches to the weak conscience. . . .

3. Such is the defilement from which the bath of the Jews cleansed. But the bath of grace does not clean the body or the weak conscience, but the real uncleanness which has introduced defilement into the soul as well as into the body. For it does not make those who have touched dead bodies clean, but those who have set their hand to dead works. If anyone is effeminate, or a fornicator, or an idolater, or a doer of whatever wrong you

please, or if he be full of all the wickedness there is among humanity, if he should fall into this pool of waters, he comes up again from the divine fountain purer than the sun's rays. And in order that you may not think that what is said is mere vain boasting, hear Paul speaking of the power of the bath, "Be not deceived: neither idolaters, nor fornicators, nor adulterers, nor effeminate, nor abusers of themselves with men, nor covetous, not drunkards, not revilers, not extortionists shall inherit the kingdom of God." And what does this have to do with what has been spoken? One might ask, "Prove the question whether the power of the bath thoroughly cleanses all these things." Hear therefore what follows: "And such were some of you, but you were washed, but you were sanctified, but you were justified in the name of the Lord Jesus Christ, and in the spirit of our God." We promise to show you that they who approach the bath become clean from all fornication: but the Word has shown more, that they have become not only clean, but both holy and just, for it does not say only "you were washed," but also "you were sanctified and were justified." What could be more strange than this, when without effort, exertion, and good works, righteousness is produced? For such is the great mercy of the Divine gift that it makes human beings just without this exertion. . . . One also might ask why it is not called a bath of remission of sins, nor a bath of cleansing, if the bath takes away all our sins? Why is it instead called a bath of regeneration? This is because it does not simply take away our sins, nor simply cleanse us from our faults, but cleanses us as though we were born again. For it creates and fashions us anew, though it does not form us again out of earth, but it creates us out of another element, namely, of the nature of water. For it does not simply wipe the vessel clean, but entirely remolds it again. For that which is wiped clean, even if it is cleaned with care, has traces of its former condition, and bears the remains of its defilement. But that which falls into the new mold, and is renewed by means of the flames, laying aside all uncleanness, comes forth from the furnace, and sends forth the same brilliancy with things newly formed. As therefore anyone who takes and recasts a golden statue which has been tarnished by time, smoke, dust, rust, restores it to us thoroughly cleansed and glistening, so too this nature of ours, rusted with the rust of sin, and having gathered much smoke from our faults, and having lost its beauty, which he had from the beginning bestowed upon it from himself, God has taken and cast anew, and throwing it into the waters as into a mold, and instead of fire sending forth the grace of the Spirit, then brings us forth with much brightness, renewed, and made afresh, to rival the beams of the sun, having crushed the old man, and having fashioned a new man, more brilliant than the former.

NPNF 1.9, ed. Philip Schaff. Reprint, Peabody, MA: Hendrickson, 1994.

Augustine of Hippo (354–430)
Enchiridion

Perhaps no other theologian has had as much influence on the Western church as Augustine. A "Doctor" of the West, he remains of significance not only for Roman Catholics but Protestants as well. Best known for his spiritual autobiography *Confessions,* he also authored numerous treatises against the Manicheans, the Pelagians, and the Donatists, addressing issues such as the Trinity, free will, grace, predestination, and just war, among others. The *Enchiridion,* or *Handbook,* is intended to explain the basics of Christian living. This selection demonstrates Augustine's reasoning for infant baptism: the baptized died to sin. For the infant, it was a death to original sin only, whereas for the adult, it was death to original sin and sins committed prior to the baptism.

Chapter Forty-Three

For from the infant newly born to the old man bent with age, as there is none shut out from baptism, so there is none who in baptism does not die to sin. But infants die only to original sin; those who are older die also to all the sins which their evil lives have added to the sin which they brought with them.

NPNF 1.3, ed. Philip Schaff. Reprint, Peabody, MA: Hendrickson, 1994.

Augustine of Hippo (354–430)
On Baptism against the Donatists

The Donatists, named after Donatus, had separated themselves from the remainder of the Christian community in the aftermath of Roman Emperor Diocletian's persecution of the church. The ruler had insisted that the Christian Scriptures be surrendered to authorities. Many bishops had acquiesced, and were termed traitors by Donatus. His followers contended that churches in which these traitors were pastors, and those congregations in fellowship with them, were stained by the grave sin of denying the Savior. Consequently, they concluded that membership in these communities of faith invalidated the sacrament of baptism. In other words, the rite of initiation was appropriately done only within a Donatist church. The following excerpts are from Augustine's polemic against that view of baptism.

Central to his argument was the idea that there are two components to salvation, which he took from Jesus' statement that to enter the Kingdom of God one must be born of water and of the spirit. The first of these corresponds to water baptism, and the second to conversion of the heart. He contended that one must have experienced both acts to be truly converted. However, Augustine did make allowances for exceptional circumstances. For example, when Jesus promised the thief on the cross next to him that he would be in paradise that very day, the thief was not baptized. However, he was prohibited by the circumstance rather than willful rejection of what was proper.

Despite a few isolated exceptions, baptism was essential for salvation, though it did not produce salvation in itself. As we have seen, this was also the view of Ambrose of Milan. One could be baptized, but not converted. Augustine cites the Donatist as an example. While the Donatist has been baptized, he or she would not be converted. Once the conversion of the heart took place, the prior baptism would be considered valid, and therefore the person would not need to be rebaptized. This argument led Augustine to his conclusion concerning infant baptism, which he identifies as corresponding to circumcision. Though the child is unaware of a need to place one's faith in Christ, he does not need rebaptism once he comes to an understanding of Christianity and willfully accepts it. In fact, the baptism of the infant removed the stain of original sin.

The most important component of this selection is Augustine's insistence that baptism is a sacrament of Christ, and not of the church. Despite this fact, he still insisted that one could not be rightly related to God without right relation to the Christian community. Here one finds a selective use of Cyprian of Carthage. The Donatists appealed to Cyprian's insistence that the sacraments are valid only within the one, true church. Augustine rejected this, and instead accepted Cyprian's idea of the necessity of membership within the proper community of faith. While he accepted the validity of the Donatists' baptism—because it was in fact the baptism of Christ—he asserted that membership in their congregation was sin.

Augustine's basic contention was that there was no need to rebaptize Donatists who wished to join the Catholic Christian community because baptism belongs solely to Christ. While required for entrance into the church, the sacrament ultimately was an individual commitment to Christ, and not to the community.

Book One

18. What if someone approached baptism in deceit? Were that person's sins remitted, or were they not? . . . If they [the Donatists] say they were not remitted, I ask whether, if he should afterwards confess his sin with contrition of heart and true sorrow, it would be judged that he ought to be baptized again. And if it is mere madness to assert this, then let them confess that a man can be baptized with the true baptism of Christ, and that yet his heart, persisting in malice or sacrilege, may not allow remission of sins to be given; and so let them understand that men may be baptized in communions severed from the Church, in which Christ's baptism is given and received in the said celebration of the sacrament, but that it will only then be of avail for the remission of sins, when the recipient, being reconciled to the unity of the Church, is purged from the sacrilege of deceit, by which his sins were retained, and their remission prevented. For, as in the case of him who had approached the sacrament in deceit there is no second baptism, but he is purged by faithful discipline and truthful confession, which he could not be without baptism, so that what was given before becomes then powerful to work his salvation, when the former deceit is done away by the truthful confession; so also in the case of the man who, while an enemy to the peace and love of Christ, received in any heresy or schism the baptism of Christ, which the schismatics in question had not lost from among them, though by his sacrilege his sins were not remitted, yet, when he corrects his error, and comes over to the communion and unity of the Church, he ought not to be again baptized: because by his very reconciliation to the peace of the Church he receives this benefit, that the sacrament now begins in unity to be of avail for the remission of his sins, which could not so avail him as received in schism.

19. But which is the worse, not to be baptized at all, or to be twice bap-tized, it is difficult to decide. I see, indeed, which is more repugnant and abhorrent to men's feelings; but when I have recourse to that divine bal-ance, in which the weight of things is determined, not by man's feelings, but by the authority of God, I find a statement by our Lord on either side. For he said to Peter, "He who is washed has no need of washing a second time;" and to Nicodemus, "Except a man be born of water and of the Spirit, he cannot enter into the kingdom of God." What is the purport of the more secret determination of God, it is perhaps difficult for men like us to learn; but as far as the mere words are concerned, any one may see what a difference there is between "has no need of washing," and "cannot enter into the kingdom of heaven." The Church, lastly, herself holds as her tradition, that without baptism she cannot admit a man to her altar at all; but since it is allowed that one who has been rebaptized may be ad-mitted after penance, surely this plainly proves that his baptism is consid-ered valid. . . .

Book Three

19. Nor is it material, when we are considering the question of the gen-uineness and holiness of the sacrament, "what the recipient of the sacra-ment believes, and with what faith he is imbued." It is of the very highest consequence as regards the entrance into salvation, but is wholly immate-rial as regards the question of the sacrament. For it is quite possible that a man may be possessed of the genuine sacrament and a corrupted faith, as it is possible that he may hold the words of the creed in their integrity, and yet entertain an erroneous belief about the Trinity, or the resurrection, or any other point. For it is no slight matter, even within the Catholic Church itself, to hold a faith entirely consistent with the truth about even God himself, to say nothing of any of his creatures. Is it then to be main-tained, that if any one who has been baptized within the Catholic Church itself should afterwards, in the course of reading, or by listening to instruc-tion, or by quiet argument, find out, through God's own revelation, that he had before believed otherwise than he ought, it is requisite that he should therefore be baptized afresh? But what carnal and natural man is

there who does not stray through the vain conceits of his own heart, and picture God's nature to himself to be such as he has imagined out of his carnal sense, and differ from the true conception of God as far as vanity from truth? Most truly, indeed, speaks the apostle, filled with the light of truth: "The natural man," he says, "does not receive the things of the Spirit of God." And yet herein he was speaking of men whom he himself shows to have been baptized. For he says to them, "Was Paul crucified for you, or were ye baptized in the name of Paul?" These men had therefore the sacrament of baptism; and yet, inasmuch as their wisdom was of the flesh, what could they believe about God otherwise than according to the perception of their flesh, according to which "the natural man does not receive the things of the Spirit of God?" To such he says: "I could not speak unto you as unto spiritual, but as unto carnal, even as unto babes in Christ. I have fed you with milk, and not with meat: for to this point you were not able to bear it, neither yet now are you able. For you are yet carnal." For such are carried about with every wind of doctrine, of which kind he says, "That we be no more children, tossed to and fro, and carried about with every wind of doctrine."

20. Accordingly, if Marcion consecrated the sacrament of baptism with the words of the gospel, "In the name of the Father, and of the Son, and of the Holy Spirit," the sacrament was complete, although his faith expressed under the same words, seeing that he held opinions not taught by the Catholic truth, was not complete, but stained with the falsity of fables. For under these same words, "In the name of the Father, and of the Son, and of the Holy Spirit," not Marcion only, or Valentinus, or Arius, or Eunomius, but the carnal babes of the church themselves (to whom the apostle said, "I could not speak unto you as unto spiritual, but as unto carnal"), if they could be individually asked for an accurate exposition of their opinions, would probably show a diversity of opinions as numerous as the persons who held them, "for the natural man does not receive the things of the Spirit of God." Can it, however, be said on this account that they do not receive the complete sacrament? Or that, if they shall advance, and correct the vanity of their carnal opinions, they must seek again what they had received? Each man receives after the fashion of his own faith; yet how much does he obtain under the guidance of that mercy of God, in the confident assurance of which the same apostle says, "If in anything you are otherwise minded, God shall reveal even this unto you"?

29. With regard to the objection brought against Cyprian, that the catechumens who were seized in martyrdom, and slain for Christ's name's sake, received a crown even without baptism, I do not quite see what it has to do with the matter, unless, indeed, they urged that heretics could much more be admitted with baptism to Christ's kingdom, to which catechumens were admitted without it, since he himself has said, "Except a man be born of water and of the Spirit, he cannot enter into the kingdom of God." Now, in this matter I do not hesitate for a moment to place the Catholic catechumen, who is burning with love for God, before the baptized heretic; nor yet do we thereby do dishonor to the sacrament of baptism which the latter has already received, the former not as yet; nor do we consider that the sacrament of the catechumen is to be preferred to the sacrament of baptism, when we acknowledge that some catechumens are better and more faithful than some baptized persons. . . . But as baptism is wanting to a good catechumen to his receiving the kingdom of heaven, so true conversion is wanting to a bad man though baptized. For he who said, "Except a man be born of water and of the Spirit, he cannot enter into the kingdom of God," said also himself, "Except your righteousness shall exceed the righteousness of the scribes and Pharisees, you shall in no case enter into the kingdom of heaven." For that the righteousness of the catechumens might not feel secure, it is written, "Except a man be born again of water and of the Spirit, he cannot enter into the kingdom of God." And again, that the unrighteousness of the baptized might not feel secure because they had received baptism, it is written, "Except your righteousness shall exceed the righteousness of the scribes and Pharisees, you shall in no case enter into the kingdom of heaven." The one were too little without the other; the two make perfect the heir of that inheritance. As, then, we ought not to deprecate a man's righteousness, which begins to exist before he is joined to the Church, . . . so neither ought we to deprecate the sacrament of baptism, even though it has been received outside the Church. But since it is of no avail for salvation unless he who has baptism indeed in full perfection be incorporated into the Church, correcting also his own depravity, let us therefore correct the error of the heretics, that we may recognize what in them is not their own but Christ's.

30. That the place of baptism is sometimes supplied by martyrdom is supported by an argument by no means trivial, which the blessed Cyprian adduces from the thief, to whom, though he was not baptized, it was yet said,

"Today you will be with me in Paradise." On considering which, again and again, I find that not only martyrdom for the sake of Christ may supply what was wanting of baptism, but also faith and conversion of heart, if recourse may not be had to the celebration of the mystery of baptism for want of time. For neither was that thief crucified for the name of Christ, but as the reward of his own deeds; nor did he suffer because he believed, but he believed while suffering. It was shown, therefore, in the case of that thief, how great is the power, even without the visible sacrament of baptism, of what the apostle says, "With the heart man believes unto righteousness, and with the mouth confession is made unto salvation." But the want is supplied invisibly only when the administration of baptism is prevented, not by contempt for religion, but by the necessity of the moment. . . .

31. But what is the precise value of the sanctification of the sacrament (which that thief did not receive, not from any want of will on his part, but because it was unavoidably omitted) and what is the effect on a man of its material application, it is not easy to say. Still, had it not been of the greatest value, the Lord would not have received the baptism of a servant. But since we must look at it in itself, without entering upon the question of the salvation of the recipient, which it is intended to work, it shows clearly enough that both in the bad, and in those who renounce the world in word and not in deed, it is itself complete, though they cannot receive salvation unless they amend their lives. But as in the thief, to whom the material administration of the sacrament was necessarily wanting, the salvation was complete, because it was spiritually present through his piety, so, when the sacrament itself is present, salvation is complete, if what the thief possessed be unavoidably wanting. And this is the firm tradition of the universal Church, in respect of the baptism of infants, who certainly are as yet unable "with the heart to believe unto righteousness, and with the mouth to make confession unto salvation," as the thief could do; nay, who even, by crying and moaning when the mystery is performed upon them, raise their voices in opposition to the mysterious words, and yet no Christian will say that they are baptized to no purpose.

32. And if any one seek for divine authority in this matter, though what is held by the whole Church, and that not as instituted by Councils, but as a matter of invariable custom, is rightly held to have been handed down by apostolic authority, still we can form a true conjecture of the value of the sacrament of baptism in the case of infants, from the parallel of circumcision, which was received by God's earlier people, and before receiving which

Abraham was justified, as Cornelius also was enriched with the gift of the Holy Spirit before he was baptized. Yet the apostle says of Abraham himself, that "he received the sign of circumcision, a seal of the righteousness of the faith," having already believed in his heart, so that "it was counted unto him for righteousness." Why, therefore, was it commanded him that he should circumcise every male child in order on the eighth day, though it could not yet believe with the heart, that it should be counted unto it for righteousness, because the sacrament in itself was of great avail? And this was made manifest by the message of an angel in the case of Moses' son; for when he was carried by his mother, being yet uncircumcised, it was required, by manifest present peril, that he should be circumcised, and when this was done, the danger of death was removed. As therefore in Abraham the justification of faith came first, and circumcision was added afterwards as the seal of faith; so in Cornelius the spiritual sanctification came first in the gift of the Holy Spirit, and the sacrament of regeneration was added afterwards in the bath of baptism. And as in Isaac, who was circumcised on the eighth day after his birth, the seal of this righteousness of faith was given first, and afterwards, as he imitated the faith of his father, the righteousness itself followed as he grew up, of which the seal had been given before when he was an infant; so in infants, who are baptized, the sacrament of regeneration is given first, and if they maintain a Christian piety, conversion also in the heart will follow, of which the mysterious sign had gone before in the outward body. And as in the thief the gracious goodness of the Almighty supplied what had been wanting in the sacrament of baptism, because it had been missing not from pride or contempt, but from want of opportunity; so in infants who die baptized, we must believe that the same grace of the Almighty supplies the want, that, not from perversity of will, but from insufficiency of age, they can neither believe with the heart unto righteousness, nor make confession with the mouth unto salvation. Therefore, when others take the vows for them, that the celebration of the sacrament may be complete in their behalf, it is unquestionably of avail for their dedication to God, because they cannot answer for themselves. But if another were to answer for one who could answer for himself, it would not be of the same avail. In accordance with which rule, we find in the gospel what strikes every one as natural when he reads it, "He is of age, he shall speak for himself."

33. By all these considerations it is proved that the sacrament of baptism is one thing, the conversion of the heart another; but that man's salvation is made complete through the two together. Nor are we to suppose that, if one

of these be wanting, it necessarily follows that the other is wanting also; because the sacrament may exist in the infant without the conversion of the heart; and this was found to be possible without the sacrament in the case of the thief, God in either case filling up what was involuntarily wanting. But when either of these requisites is wanting intentionally, then the man is responsible for the omission. And baptism may exist when the conversion of the heart is wanting; but, with respect to such conversion, it may indeed be found when baptism has not been received, but never when it has been despised. Nor can there be said in any way to be a turning of the heart to God when the sacrament of God is treated with contempt. Therefore we are right in censuring, anathematizing, abhorring, and abominating the perversity of heart shown by heretics; yet it does not follow that they have not the sacrament of the gospel, because they have not what makes it of avail. Wherefore, when they come to the true faith, and by penitence seek remission of their sins, we are not flattering or deceiving them, when we instruct them by heavenly discipline for the kingdom of heaven, correcting and reforming in them their errors and perverseness, to the intent that we may by no means do violence to what is sound in them, nor, because of man's fault, declare that anything which he may have in him from God is either valueless or faulty.

NPNF 1.4, ed. Philip Schaff. Reprint, Peabody, MA: Hendrickson, 1994.

ADDITIONAL READINGS

Aland, K. *Did the Early Church Baptize Infants?* Philadelphia: Westminster, 1963.

Ferguson, E., ed. *Conversion, Catechumenate, and Baptism in the Early Church,* Studies in Early Christianity, vol. 11. New York: Garland, 1993.

Finn, T. M. *Early Christian Baptism and the Catechumenate.* Collegeville, MN: Liturgical, 1992.

Hamman, A. *Baptism: Ancient Liturgies and Patristic Texts.* New York: Alba House, 1967.

Harmless, W. *Augustine and the Catechumenate.* Collegeville, MN: Liturgical, 1995.

Jeremias, J. *Infant Baptism in the First Four Centuries.* Philadelphia: Westminster, 1960.

Jeremias, J. *The Origins of Infant Baptism.* London: SCM, 1963.

Riley, H. *Christian Initiation.* Washington, DC: Catholic University of America Press, 1974.

Weil, L. *Sacraments and Liturgy: The Outward Signs.* Oxford: Blackwell, 1983.

Yarnold, E. *The Awe-Inspiring Rites of Initiation.* 2nd ed. Edinburgh: Clark, 1994.

CHAPTER 2

Assembling the Community

Worship in the Early Church

🌿

The Christian community believed it important to assemble for instruction in the matters of their faith and for the corporate worship of God. Because the earliest Christians were adherents to first-century Judaism, they gathered on the Jewish Sabbath, as they had prior to their conversion to Christianity. In addition, these Christians, or the "church" (from the Greek *ecclesia,* or "called out ones") as they were now called, also met with one another on Sunday. They began to call Sunday the Lord's Day because Jesus was resurrected from the dead on the first day of the week. His followers met to worship him on this day to celebrate his victory over death and provision for salvation.

As time progressed, the components of the worship service became more standardized. The constituent elements of Christian worship were collectively called the liturgy, from the Greek word for service. The order of the worship service would vary from one particular congregation to another. However, some parts would be nearly universal: prayers for one another and those outside the community, reading from the Scriptures, preaching or expounding what had been read, practical instruction concerning right Christian living, the singing of hymns, and sharing in the Eucharist, or Lord's Supper.

One important point of disagreement regarded the use of music in worship. Both Clement of Alexandria in the late second and early third centuries and John Chrysostom of Constantinople in the late fourth century were opposed to musical instruments in the assembly. For them both, such entertainments aroused earthly as opposed to heavenly passions. We also find Basil of Caesarea in the fourth century defending the singing of psalms against those who objected to the practice.

One theme that runs through all of the following selections is the importance of the sincerity of the worshipper. Merely attending the service out of a sense of duty was considered useless. The purpose was to effect a changed life. Because sincere participation in the assembly produced spiritual benefits, the gathering together of believers on the day of Jesus' resurrection was considered an essential part of life and practice in the early church.

Ignatius of Antioch (35–107)

To the Magnesians

One of the Apostolic Fathers, Ignatius was bishop of Antioch during the reign of Roman Emperor Trajan, who ruled from 98 to 117. He was arrested during Trajan's persecution of the Christians and taken to Rome for execution. En route to his martyrdom, he penned seven letters, including the one cited here to the Christians in the city of Magnesia in Southern Asia Minor. This is one of the earliest non-canonical writings extant, and demonstrates a high view of the office of bishop, who could protect the community from heresy and division.

For Ignatius, corporate Christian worship was to be done on Sunday, which was called the Lord's Day. Worship was to be treated as a festival in celebration of Christ's resurrection on the first day of the week. He considered this day to be the most important day of the week. With reference to the Jewish background of Christianity, Ignatius did not consider Sunday to be a "Christian Sabbath," but rather an extension of the Sabbath, which was to be observed by meditation on the Scriptures, rather than physical rest.

Chapter Nine

If, then, those who were conversant with the ancient Scriptures came to newness of hope, expecting the coming of Christ, as the Lord teaches us when he says, "If you had believed Moses, you would have believed me, for he wrote of me"; and again, "Your father Abraham rejoiced to see My day, and he saw it, and was glad; for before Abraham was, I am." "How shall we be able to live without him? The prophets were his servants, and foresaw him by the

Spirit, and waited for him as their Teacher, and expected him as their Lord and Savior, saying, "He will come and save us." Let us therefore no longer keep the Sabbath after the Jewish manner, and rejoice in days of idleness; for "he that does not work, let him not eat." For the holy Scriptures say, "In the sweat of your face you will eat your bread." But let every one of you keep the Sabbath after a spiritual manner, rejoicing in meditation on the law, not in relaxation of the body, admiring the workmanship of God, and not eating things prepared the day before, nor using lukewarm drinks, and walking within a prescribed space, nor finding delight in dancing and plaudits which have no sense in them. And after the observance of the Sabbath, let every friend of Christ keep the Lord's Day as a festival, the resurrection-day, the queen and chief of all the days of the week.

ANF 1, ed. A. Cleveland Coxe. Reprint, Peabody, MA: Hendrickson, 1994.

The Didache (Early Second Century)

In this selection of the *Didache,* or Teaching of the Lord, the anonymous writers of this church manual instructed the Christian community to assemble every Sunday, or Lord's Day. At the assembly they were to break bread—presumably the feast known as the agape—which would include celebration of the Eucharist. A significant component to Christian worship in the *Didache* was the unity of the believers. Here we find instruction that a member who was not in right fellowship with another member should not attend worship until there had been reconciliation.

Chapter Fourteen

But every Lord's Day gather yourselves together, and break bread, and give thanksgiving after having confessed your transgressions, that your sacrifice may be pure. But let no one that is at variance with his fellow Christian come together with you, until they be reconciled, that your sacrifice may not be profaned. For this is that which was spoken by the Lord, "In every place and time offer to me a pure sacrifice; for I am a great King, says the Lord, and my name is wonderful among the nations."

ANF 7, ed. A. Cleveland Coxe. Reprint, Peabody, MA: Hendrickson, 1994.

Justin *Martyr* (*110–165*)

First Apology

As one will recall from chapter 1, Justin was one of the most significant of the second-century Christian apologists, known for his defense of Christianity against Judaism and paganism. This selection affords the reader a vivid glimpse into second-century Christian worship and its background. Worship consisted of reading the Scriptures, explaining what had been read, instructing the listeners in proper living, praying, and sharing in the Eucharist. Justin says this public gathering took place on Sunday for two reasons. First, it was the day on which God created the world. Second, it was the day of Jesus' resurrection from the dead. Worship was not limited to the physical gathering of believers, however. Some members would be unable to attend the service because of health or other legitimate reasons. For their benefit, the deacons took the elements of the Lord's Supper to them. The worship of the church therefore extended beyond the meeting place, emphasizing the importance of the community of faith for early Christians.

Chapter Sixty-Seven

And we afterwards continually remind each other of these things. And the wealthy among us help the needy; and we always keep together; and for all things wherewith we are supplied, we bless the Maker of all through his Son Jesus Christ, and through the Holy Spirit. And on the day called Sunday, all who live in cities or in the country gather together to one place, and the memoirs of the apostles or the writings of the prophets are read, as long as time permits; then, when the reader has ceased, the overseer verbally instructs, and exhorts to the imitation of these good things. Then we all rise together and pray, and, as we before said, when our prayer is ended, bread and wine and water are brought, and the overseer in like manner offers prayers and thanksgivings, according to his ability, and the people assent, saying Amen; and there is a distribution to each, and a participation of that over which thanks have been given, and to those who are absent a portion is sent by the deacons. And they who are well to do, and willing, give what each thinks fit; and what is collected is deposited with the overseer, who provides for the orphans and widows and those who, through sickness or any other cause, are in want, and those who are in bonds and the strangers sojourning among us, and in a word takes care of all who are in need. But Sunday is the day on which we all hold our common assembly, because it is the first day on which God, having wrought a change in the darkness and matter, made the world; and Jesus Christ our Savior on the same day rose from the dead. For he was crucified on the day before that of Saturn (Saturday); and on the day after that of Saturn, which is the day of the Sun, having appeared to his apostles and disciples, he taught them these things, which we have submitted to you also for your consideration.

ANF 1, ed. A. Cleveland Coxe. Reprint, Peabody, MA: Hendrickson, 1994.

Clement of Alexandria (150–215)
The Instructor

Clement became head of the Catechetical School in Alexandria around 190, after receiving a classical education in philosophy and further study in Christianity. He is known for his typological interpretation of Scripture and his understanding of gnosis, or secret knowledge, as the goal of Christian perfection.

The subject of the following selection is the use of musical instruments in Christian worship. An atmosphere of revelry in the church was unacceptable, he says, because it aroused the emotions and led participants into inappropriate behavior. Music led to seduction and a desire for sensation. Banqueting prompted its participants to seek a type of pleasure that was not proper for Christians.

Clement interpreted the Psalmists' call to praise God in an interesting fashion. The musical instruments spoken of were not to be taken literally, but figuratively. For example, the lyre was the mouth that was struck by the Spirit. The cymbal was the tongue. The only appropriate instrument of worship was the person. The selection exhibits Clement's style of biblical interpretation.

Book Two, Chapter Four

Let revelry keep away from our rational entertainments, and foolish vigils, too, that revel in intemperance. For revelry is an inebriating pipe, the chain of an amatory bridge, that is, of sorrow. And let love, and intoxication, and senseless passions, be removed from our choir. Burlesque singing is the boon companion of drunkenness. A night spent over drink invites drunkenness, rouses lust, and is audacious in deeds of shame. For if people occupy their time with pipes, and psalteries, and choirs, and dances, and Egyptian clapping of hands, and such disorderly frivolities, they become quite immodest and intractable, beat on cymbals and drums, and make a noise on instruments of delusion; for plainly such a banquet, as seems to me, is a theatre of drunkenness. For the apostle decrees that, "putting off the works of darkness, we should put on the armor of light, walking honestly as in the day, not spending our time in rioting and drunkenness, in chambering and wantonness." Let the pipe be resigned to the shepherds, and the flute to the superstitious who are engrossed in idolatry. For, in truth, such instruments are to be banished from the temperate banquet, being more suitable to beasts than men, and the more irrational portion of mankind. For we have heard of stags being charmed by the pipe, and seduced by music into the toils, when hunted by the huntsmen. And when mares are being covered, a tune is played on the flute— a nuptial song, as it were. And every improper sight and sound, to speak in a word, and every shameful sensation of licentiousness—which, in truth, is privation of sensation—must by all means be excluded; and we must be on our guard against whatever pleasure titillates eye and ear, and effeminates. . . .

The Spirit, distinguishing from such revelry the divine service, sings, "Praise him with the sound of trumpet"; for with sound of trumpet he shall raise the dead. "Praise him on the psaltery"; for the tongue is the psaltery of the Lord. "And praise him on the lyre." By the lyre is meant the mouth struck by the Spirit, as it were by a plectrum. "Praise with the cymbal and the dance," refers to the Church meditating on the resurrection of the dead in the resounding skin. "Praise him on the chords and organ." Our body he calls an organ, and its nerves are the strings, by which it has received harmonious tension, and when struck by the Spirit, it gives forth human voices. "Praise him on the clashing cymbals." He calls the tongue the cymbal of the mouth, which resounds with the pulsation of the lips. Therefore he cried to humanity, "Let every breath praise the Lord," because he cares for every breathing thing which he has made. For man is truly a pacific instrument; while other instruments, if you investigate, you will find to be warlike, inflaming to lusts, or kindling up amours, or rousing wrath.

ANF 2, ed. A. Cleveland Coxe. Reprint, Peabody, MA: Hendrickson, 1994.

Tertullian of Carthage (160–212)

Apology

The North African apologist's purpose in the following selection was to explain the activities associated with Christian worship. Christianity's opponents had deemed Christians to be dangerous to society, as demonstrated by their private and secretive assemblies. The author described what happened at a Christian worship service. He emphasized that the worshippers prayed for the emperor and all who were in authority, as well as other members of society. They also prayed for peace in the world and the good of society. The pastor read and expounded the Scriptures, and exhorted the people to live good lives.

After the explanation of the Scripture, the people gathered for the agape, or love feast. This was a meal in which the church shared their blessings with one another and with those in need. The feast of the agape was modest, he said, and not a drunken party filled with gluttony. Participants ate only what was needed to satisfy hunger and drank moderately. The consummation of the feast was an offering, probably referring to the offering of the Eucharist. Hymns from participants followed, and the worship was concluded as it began, with a prayer.

Chapter Thirty-Nine

I shall at once go on, then, to exhibit the peculiarities of the Christian society, that, as I have refuted the evil charged against it, I may point out its positive good. We are a body knit together as such by a common religious profession, by unity of discipline, and by the bond of a common hope. We meet together as an assembly and congregation, that, offering up prayer to God as with united force, we may wrestle with him in our supplications. This violence God delights in. We pray, too, for the emperors, for their ministers and for all in authority, for the welfare of the world, for the prevalence of peace, for the delay of the final consummation. We assemble to read our sacred writings, if any peculiarity of the times makes either forewarning or reminiscence needful. However it be in that respect, with the sacred words we nourish our faith, we animate our hope, we make our confidence more steadfast; and no less by inculcations of God's precepts we confirm good habits. In the same place also exhortations are made, rebukes and sacred censures are administered. For with a great gravity is the work of judging carried on among us, as befits those who feel assured that they are in the sight of God; and you have the most notable example of judgment to come when any one has sinned so grievously as to require his severance from us in prayer, in the congregation and in all sacred intercourse. The tried men of our elders preside over us, obtaining that honor not by purchase, but by established character. There is no buying and selling of any sort in the things of God. Though we have our treasure-chest, it is not made up of purchase-money, as of a religion that has its price. On the monthly day, if he likes, each puts in a small donation; but only if it be his pleasure, and only if he be able: for there is no compulsion; all is voluntary. These gifts are, as it were, piety's deposit fund. For they are not taken thence and spent on feasts, and drinking-bouts, and eating-houses, but to support and bury poor people, to supply the wants of boys and girls destitute of means and parents, and of old persons confined now to the house; such, too, as have suffered shipwreck; and if there happen to be any in the mines, or banished to the islands, or shut up in the prisons, for nothing but their fidelity to the cause of God's Church, they become the nurslings of their confession. But it is mainly the deeds of a love so noble that lead many to put a brand upon us. . . . Our feast explains itself by its name. The Greeks call it agape, i.e., affection. Whatever it costs, our outlay in the name of piety is gain, since with the good things of the feast we benefit the needy; not as it is with you, do parasites aspire to the glory of satisfying their licentious propensities, selling themselves for a belly-feast to all disgraceful treatment,—but as it is with God himself, a peculiar respect is shown to the lowly. If the object of our feast be good, in the light of that consider its further regulations. As it is an act of religious service, it permits no vileness or immodesty. The participants, before reclining, taste first of prayer to God. As much is eaten as satisfies the cravings of hunger; as much is drunk as befits the chaste. They say it is enough, as those who remember that even during the night they have to worship God; they talk as those who know that the Lord is one of their auditors. After manual ablution, and the bringing in of lights, each is asked to stand forth and sing, as he can, a hymn to God, either one from the holy Scriptures or one of his own composing,—a proof of the measure of our drinking. As the feast commenced with prayer, so with prayer it is closed. We go from it, not like troops of mischief-doers, nor bands of vagabonds, nor to break out into licentious acts, but to have as much care of our modesty and chastity as if we had been at a school of virtue rather than a banquet. Give the congregation of the Christians its due, and hold it unlawful, if it is like assemblies of the illicit sort: by all means let it be condemned, if any complaint can be validly laid against it, such as lies against secret factions. But who has ever suffered harm from our assemblies? We are in our congregations just what we are when separated from each other; we are as a community what we are individuals; we injure nobody, we trouble nobody. When the upright, when the virtuous meet together, when the pious, when the pure assemble in congregation, you ought not to call that a faction, but a curia [i.e., the court of God].

ANF 3, ed. A. Cleveland Coxe. Reprint, Peabody, MA: Hendrickson, 1994.

Apostolic Constitutions (Fourth Century)

This selection of the important compilation of church orders from the end of the fourth century employed the analogy of a ship to illustrate its message concerning Christian worship. The bishop was analogous to the ship's captain and the deacons to the mariners on the ship. The building in which the church met was to resemble a ship. Like passengers, participants in worship services were to have their own respective places. The bishop was to be seated centrally, with the presbyters seated around him. The deacons were to be standing nearby to assist the bishops and presbyters, and to help manage the participants. Deacons were responsible for ensuring that worshippers did not act inappropriately by whispering, nodding off, and the like. Women and men stood separately from one another. Children and the elderly had their respective places to be seated.

The service of worship consisted of two readings from the Old Testament Scriptures followed by the singing of a hymn. Next were readings from the New Testament. After the readings the presbyters took turns expounding the Scripture and exhorting the people to right living. The catechumens and penitents (i.e., those members doing penance) were then dismissed from the service before the baptized members shared in the Lord's Supper. Participants offered to one another the "Lord's kiss" and then offered the Eucharist together.

57. When you [the bishop] call an assembly of the Church as one that is the commander of a great ship, appoint the assemblies to be made with all possible skill, charging the deacons as mariners to prepare places for the brethren as for passengers, with all due care and decency. And first, let the building be long, with its head to the east, with its vestries on both sides at the east end, and so it will be like a ship. In the middle let the bishop's throne be placed, and on each side of him let the presbytery sit down; and let the deacons stand near at hand, in close and small girt garments, for they are like the mariners and managers of the ship: with regard to these, let the laity sit on the other side, with all quietness and good order. And let the women sit by themselves, they also keeping silence. In the middle, let the reader stand upon some high place: let him read the books of Moses, of Joshua the son of Nun, of the Judges, and of the Kings and of the Chronicles, and those written after the return from the captivity; and besides these, the books of Job and of Solomon, and of the sixteen prophets. But when there have been two lessons severally read, let some other person sing the hymns of David, and let the people join at the conclusions of the verses. Afterwards let our Acts be read, and the Letters of Paul our fellow-worker, which he sent to the churches under the conduct of the Holy Spirit; and afterwards let a deacon or a presbyter read the Gospels, both those which I Matthew and John have delivered to you, and those which the fellow-workers of Paul received and left to you, Luke and Mark. And while the Gospel is read, let all the presbyters and deacons, and all the people, stand up in great silence; for it is written: "Be silent, and hear, O Israel." And again: "But do you stand there, and hear." In the next place, let the presbyters one by one, not all together, exhort the people, and the bishop in the last place, as being the commander. Let the porters stand at the entries of the men, and observe them. Let the deaconesses also stand at those of the women, like shipmen. For the same description and pattern was both in the tabernacle of the testimony and in the temple of God. But if any one be found sitting out of his place, let him be rebuked by the deacon, as a manager of the ship, and be removed into the place proper for him; for the Church is not only like a ship, but also like a sheepfold. For as the shepherds place all the brute creatures distinctly, I mean goats and sheep, according to their kind and age, and still every one runs together, like to his like; so is it to be in the Church. Let the young persons sit by themselves, if

there be a place for them; if not, let them stand upright. But let those that are already stricken in years sit in order. For the children which stand, let their fathers and mothers take them to them. Let the younger women also sit by themselves, if there be a place for them; but if there be not, let them stand behind the women. Let those women which are married, and have children, be placed by themselves; but let the virgins, and the widows, and the elder women, stand or sit before all the rest; and let the deacon be the disposer of the places, that every one of those that comes in may go to his proper place, and may not sit at the entrance. In like manner, let the deacon oversee the people, that nobody may whisper, nor slumber, nor laugh, nor nod; for all ought in the church to stand wisely, and soberly, and attentively, having their attention fixed upon the word of the Lord. After this, let all rise up with one consent, and looking towards the east, after the catechumens and penitents are gone out, pray to God eastward, who ascended up to the heaven of heavens to the east; remembering also the ancient situation of paradise in the east, from whence the first man, when he had yielded to the persuasion of the serpent, and disobeyed the command of God, was expelled. As to the deacons, after the prayer is over, let some of them attend upon the oblation of the Eucharist, ministering to the Lord's body with fear. Let others of them watch the multitude, and keep them silent. But let that deacon who is at the high priest's hand say to the people, Let no one have any quarrel against another; let no one come in hypocrisy. Then let the men give the men, and the women give the women, the Lord's kiss. But let no one do it with deceit, as Judas betrayed the Lord with a kiss. After this let the deacon pray for the whole Church, for the whole world, and the several parts of it, and the fruits of it; for the priests and the rulers, for the high priest and the king, and the peace of the universe. After this let the high priest pray for peace upon the people, and bless them, as Moses commanded the priests to bless the people, in these words: "The Lord bless you, and keep you: the Lord make his face to shine upon you, and give you peace." Let the bishop pray for the people, and say: "Save your people, O Lord, and bless your inheritance, which you have obtained with the precious blood of your Christ, and have called a royal priesthood, and a holy nation." After this let the sacrifice follow, the people standing, and praying silently; and when the oblation has been made, let every rank by itself partake of the Lord's body and precious blood in order, and approach with reverence and holy fear, as to the body of their king. Let the women approach with their heads covered, as is becoming the order of women; but let the door be watched, lest any unbeliever, or one not yet initiated, come in.

ANF 7, ed. A. Cleveland Coxe. Reprint, Peabody, MA: Hendrickson, 1994.

Cyril of Jerusalem (315–386)
Catechetical Lecture 23

As part of his catechetical lectures delivered at the beginning of his tenure as pastor of the Jerusalem church, Cyril explained the meaning of the various components of a worship service for the catechumens. He described how the service began with the overseer and presbyters washing their hands. This act was a symbol to the worshippers of the need for washing of sin. The people were then to greet one another with a "holy kiss," symbolic of the unity of the Christian community. Next in the liturgy the overseers called for the worshippers to lift up sincere hearts to the Lord. The singing of hymns followed, in preparation for the Eucharist. Whereas in the earlier selections the exposition of Scripture was central to the worship service, in Cyril sharing in the Lord's Supper was central.

2. You have seen then the Deacon who gives to the Priest water to wash, and to the Presbyters who stand round God's altar. He gave it not at all because of bodily defilement; it is not that; for we did not enter the Church at first with defiled bodies. But the washing of hands is a symbol that you ought to be pure from all sinful and unlawful deeds; for since the hands are a symbol of action, by washing them, it is evident, we represent the purity and blamelessness of our conduct. Did you not hear the blessed David opening this very mystery, and saying, "I will wash my hands in innocence, and so will compass your Altar, O Lord?" The washing therefore of hands is a symbol of immunity from sin.

3. Then the Deacon cries aloud, "Receive one another; and let us kiss one another." Think not that this kiss is of the same character with those given in public by common friends. It is not such: but this kiss blends souls one with another, and courts entire forgiveness for them. The kiss therefore is the sign that our souls are mingled together, and banish all remembrance of wrongs. For this cause Christ said, "If you are offering your gift at the altar, and there remember that your brother has something against you, leave there

your gift upon the altar, and go your way; first be reconciled to your brother, and then come and offer your gift." The kiss therefore is reconciliation, and for this reason holy: as the blessed Paul somewhere cried, saying, "Greet one another with a holy kiss"; and Peter, "with a kiss of charity."

4. After this the Priest cries aloud, "Lift up your hearts." For truly ought we in that most awful hour to have our heart on high with God, and not below, thinking of earth and earthly things. In effect therefore the Priest bids all in that hour to dismiss all cares of this life, or household anxieties, and to have their heart in heaven with the merciful God. Then you answer, "We lift them up unto the Lord": assenting to it, by your avowal. But let no one come here, who could say with his mouth, "We lift up our hearts unto the Lord," but in his thoughts have his mind concerned with the cares of this life. At all times, rather, God should be in our memory but if this is impossible by reason of human infirmity, in that hour above all this should be our earnest endeavor. . . .

7. Then having sanctified ourselves by these spiritual Hymns, we beseech the merciful God to send forth his Holy Spirit upon the gifts lying before him; that he may make the Bread the Body of Christ, and the Wine the Blood of Christ; for whatsoever the Holy Spirit has touched, is surely sanctified and changed. . . .

11. Then, after these things, we say that Prayer which the Savior delivered to his own disciples. . . .

23. Hold fast these traditions undefiled and, keep yourselves free from offence. Do not sever yourselves from the Assembly; do not deprive yourselves, through the pollution of sins, of these Holy and Spiritual Mysteries. And may the God of peace sanctify you wholly; and may your spirit, and soul, and body be preserved entire without blame at the coming of our Lord Jesus Christ.

NPNF 2.7, ed. W. Sanday. Reprint, Peabody, MA: Hendrickson, 1994.

Basil of Caesarea (330–379)

Letter 207

Basil "the Great" was one of the so-called Cappadocian Fathers, along with his younger brother Gregory of Nyssa and their mutual friend Gregory of Nazianzus. The three were originally from the area of Cappadocia in Asia

Minor. Basil, Gregory of Nazianzus, and John Chrysostom are three of the most important theologians of the church, particularly in the East. In the letter below, Basil responded to the charge that he had introduced inappropriate innovation to the church's worship by advocating the singing of psalms. He argued that singing was in fact an important component of Christian worship. The central question in worship, for Basil, was not outward style but inward sincerity and right living. The selection concludes with an admonition to his detractors that they were focusing their efforts on the inconsequential to the neglect of things of consequence. Significantly, Basil's liturgy is still used in worship today, particularly in the Coptic Orthodox Church.

3. Now as to the charge relating to the singing of psalms, in which my detractors scare the simpler folk, my reply is this. The customs which now obtain are agreeable to those of all the Churches of God. Among us the people go at night to the house of prayer, and, in distress, affliction, and continual tears, making confession to God, at last rise from their prayers and begin to sing psalms. And now, divided into two parts, they sing antiphonally with one another, thus at once confirming their study of the Gospels, and at the same time producing for themselves a heedful temper and a heart free from distraction. Afterwards they again commit the prelude of the strain to one, and the rest take it up; and so after passing the night in various psalmody, praying at intervals as the day begins to dawn, all together, as with one voice and one heart, raise the psalm of confession to the Lord, each forming for himself his own expressions of penitence. If it is for these reasons that you renounce me, you will renounce the Egyptians; you will renounce both Libyans, Thebans, Palestinians, Arabians, Phoenicians, Syrians, the dwellers by the Euphrates; in a word all those among whom vigils, prayers, and common psalmody have been held in honor.

4. But, it is alleged, these practices were not observed in the time of the great Gregory. My rejoinder is that even the Litanies which you now use were not used in his time. I do not say this to find fault with you; for my prayer would be that every one of you should live in tears and continual penitence. We, for our part, are always offering supplication for our sins, but we propitiate our God not as you do, in the words of mere man, but in the oracles of the Spirit. And what evidence have you that this custom was not followed in the time of the great Gregory? You have kept none of his customs up to the present time. Gregory did not cover his head at prayer. How could he? he was

a true disciple of the Apostle who says, "Every man praying or prophesying, having his head covered, dishonors his head." And "a man indeed ought not to cover his bead forasmuch as he is the image of God." Oaths were shunned by Gregory, that pure soul, worthy of the fellowship of the Holy Spirit, content with yes and no, in accordance with the commandment of the Lord who said, "I say unto you swear not at all." Gregory could not bear to call his brother a fool, for he stood in awe of the threat of the Lord. Passion, wrath, and bitterness never proceeded out of his mouth. Railing he hated, because it leads not to the kingdom of heaven. Envy and arrogance had been shut out of that guiltless soul. He would never have stood at the altar before being reconciled to his brother. A lie, or any word designed to slander any one, he abominated, as one who knew that lies come from the devil, and that the Lord will destroy all that utter a lie. If you have none of these things, and are clear of all, then are you truly disciples of the disciple of the Lord. If not, beware, lest in your disputes about the mode of singing psalms, you are straining at the gnat and setting at naught the greatest of the commandments.

NPNF 2.8, ed. W. Sanday. Reprint, Peabody, MA: Hendrickson, 1994.

John Chrysostom of Constantinople (347–407)
To Those Who Had Not Attended the Assembly

The selection that follows is concerned with the lax attitude of many to church attendance. Chrysostom (the "Golden-tongued") remarked that on particular days throughout the year, such as Christmas and Easter, the church was filled to overflowing. In fact, he spoke of the oppressing crowds who would show up. Other than those times, however, "not even the smallest part of that multitude is gathered together." His audience was not, as one might expect, those who were not in attendance. Rather, it was the congregation who was present. He exhorted them to be about the task of bringing others with them. They should constrain their family members and neighbors to be faithful in corporate worship. Excuses for not attending worship were to be refuted, he contended. One excuse in particular was the oppressive heat of the Constantinopolitan summer. He instructed the people to be reminded of the sufferings of others, such as the Apostle Paul and his missionary companion Silas. As they labored in prison, they sang hymns of praise to God. Those of the Jewish religion observed their Sabbath strictly, with, for Chrysostom, no eternal benefit to them. Christians should have participated in the assembly of the church even more strictly because of the spiritual benefits it provided.

Another excuse Chrysostom addressed is the need to work on Sunday. His contention was that participants would find their secular work easier as a result of worshipping. In addition, the spiritual gain one receives from sincere worship far outweighed the temporal gain one might hope to gain by working on the Lord's Day.

He did not advocate viewing attendance at church alone as beneficial. He admonished his hearers to have sincere hearts when at worship, concentrating on God rather than earthly matters. He argued that if there was no response to the instruction and exhortation at worship, attendance was useless. Worshippers should demonstrate the truth of their message by right living once they had left the gathering. In so doing, they would inspire others to attend worship with them.

2. How am I distressed, think you, when I call to mind that on the festival days the multitudes assembled resemble the broad expanse of the sea, but now not even the smallest part of that multitude is gathered together here? Where are they now who oppress us with their presence on the feast days? I look for them, and am grieved on their account when I mark what a multitude are perishing of those who are in the way of salvation, how large a loss of brethren I sustain, how few are reached by the things which concern salvation, and how the greater part of the body of the Church is like a dead and motionless carcass. "And what concern is that to us?" you say. The greatest possible concern if you pay no attention to your brethren, if you do not exhort and advise, if you put no constraint on them, and do not forcibly drag them hither, and lead them away out of their deep indolence. For you should not be useful to yourself alone, but also to many others. It is not that you should enjoy the light by yourself, but you should bring back that person who has gone astray. For what profit is a lamp if it does not give light to him who sits in darkness? What profit is a Christian when he benefits no one, neither leads any one back to virtue? Again salt is not an astringent to itself but braces up those parts of the body which have decayed, and prevents them from falling to pieces and perishing. Even so do you, since God has appointed you to be spiritual salt, bind and brace up the decayed members, that is the indolent and sordid brethren, and having rescued them from their indolence as from some form of corruption, unite them to the rest of the body of the

Church. And this is the reason why he called you leaven: for leaven also does not leaven itself, but, little though it is, it affects the whole lump however big it may be. So also do you: although you are few in number, yet be you many and powerful in faith, and in zeal towards God. As then the leaven is not weak on account of its littleness, but prevails owing to its inherent heat, and the force of its natural quality so you also will be able to bring back a far larger number than yourselves, if you will, to the same degree of zeal as your own. Now if they make the summer season their excuse: for I hear of their saying things of this kind, "the present stifling heat is excessive, the scorching sun is intolerable, we cannot bear being trampled and crushed in the crowd, and to be steaming all over with perspiration and oppressed by the heat and confined space": I am ashamed of them, believe me: for such excuses are womanish: indeed even in their case who have softer bodies, and a weaker nature, such pretexts do not suffice for justification. Nevertheless, even if it seems a disgrace to make a reply to a defense of this kind, yet is it necessary. For if they put forward such excuses as these and do not blush, much more does it behoove us not to be ashamed of replying to these things. What then am I to say to those who advance these pretexts? I would remind them of the three children in the furnace and the flame, who when they saw the fire encircling them on all sides, enveloping their mouth and their eyes and even their breath, did not cease singing that sacred and mystical hymn to God, in company with the universe, but standing in cheerfulness than they who abide in some flowery field: and together with these three children I should think it proper to remind them also of the lions which were in Babylon, and of Daniel and the den: and not of this one only but also of another den, and the prophet Jeremiah, and the mire in which he was smothered up to the neck. And emerging from these dens, I would conduct these persons who put forward heat as an excuse into the prison and exhibit Paul to them there, and Silas bound fast in the stocks, covered with bruises and wounds lacerated all over their body with a mass of stripes, yet singing praises to God at midnight and celebrating their holy fire, and the den, and amongst wild beasts, and mire, and in a prison and the stocks and amidst stripes and intolerable sufferings, never complained of any of these things but were continually uttering prayers and sacred songs with much energy and fervent zeal, whilst we who have not undergone any of their innumerable sufferings small or great, neglect our own salvation on account of a scorching sun and a little short lived heat and toil, and forsaking the assembly wander away, depraving ourselves by going to meetings which are thoroughly unwholesome? When the dew of the divine oracles is so abundant do you make heat your excuse? "The water which I will give him," says Christ "shall be in him a well of water springing up into ever-lasting life"; and again; "he that believeth on me as the Scripture has said, out of his belly shall flow rivers of living water." Tell me; when you have spiritual wets and rivers are you afraid of material heat? Now in the market place where there is so much turmoil and crowding, and scorching wind, how is it that you do not make suffocation and heat an excuse for absenting yourself? For it is impossible for you to say that there you can enjoy a cooler tempera-ture, and that all the heat is concentrated here with us—the truth is exactly the reverse; here indeed owing to the pavement floor, and to the construction of the building in other respects (for it is carried up to a vast height), the air is lighter and cooler: whereas there the sun is strong in every direction, and there is much crowding, and vapor and dust, and other things which add to discomfort far more than these. Whence it is plain that these senseless excuses are the offspring of indolence and of a supine disposition, destitute of the fire of the Holy Spirit.

3. Now these remarks of mine are not so much directed to them, as to you who do not bring them forward, do not rouse them from their indolence, and draw them to this table of salvation. Household slaves indeed when they have to discharge some service in common, summon their fellow slaves, but when you are gathering for this spiritual ministry you cause your fellow servants to be deprived of the advantage by your neglect. "But what if they do not desire it?" you say. Make them desire it by your continual importunity: for if they see you insisting upon it they certainly will desire it. Nay these things are a mere excuse and pretence. How many fathers at any rate are there here who have not their sons standing with them? Was it so difficult for you to bring hither some of your children? Whence it is dear that the absence of all the others who remain outside is due not only to their own indolence, but also to your neglect. But now at least if never before, rouse yourselves up, and let each person enter the Church accompanied by a member of his family: let them incite and urge one another to the assembly here, the father his son, the son his father, the husbands their wives and the wives their husbands, the master his slave, brother his brother, friend his friend: or rather let us not summon friends only but also enemies to this common treasury of good things. If your enemy sees your care for his welfare, he will undoubtedly re-linquish his hatred.

Say to him: "Are you not ashamed and do you not blush before the Jews who keep their Sabbath with such great strictness, and from the evening of it abstain from all work? And if they see the sun verging towards setting on the day of the Preparation they break off business, and cut short their traffic: and if any one who has been making a purchase from them, before the evening, comes in the evening bringing the price, they do not suffer themselves to take it, or to accept the money." And why do I speak of the price of market wares and transaction of business? Even if it were possible to receive a treasure they would rather lose the gain than trample on their law. Are the Jews then so strict, and this when they keep the law out of due season, and cling to an observance of it which does not profit them, but rather does them harm: and wilt you, who are superior to the shadow, to whom it has been vouchsafed to see the Sun of Righteousness, who are ranked as a citizen of the Heavenly commonwealth, wilt you not display the same zeal as those who unseasonably cleave to what is wrong, you who have been entrusted with the truth, but although you are summoned here for only a short part of the day, can you not endure to spend even this upon the hearing of the divine oracles? What kind of indulgence, I ask, could you obtain? What answer will you have to make which is reasonable and just? It is utterly impossible that one who is so indifferent and indolent should ever obtain indulgence, even if he should allege the necessities of worldly affairs ten thousand times over as an excuse. Do you not know that if you come and worship God and take part in the work which goes on here, the business you have on hand is made much easier for you? Have you worldly anxieties? Come here on that account that by the time you spend here you may win for yourself the favor of God, and so depart with a sense of security; that you may have him for your ally, that you may become invincible to the demons because you are assisted by the heavenly hand. If you have the benefit of prayers uttered by the fathers, if you take part in common prayer, if you listen to the divine oracles, if you win for yourself the aid of God, if, armed with these weapons, you then go forth, not even the devil himself will be able henceforth to look you in the face, much less wicked men who are eager to insult and malign you. But if you go from your house to the market place, and are found destitute of these weapons, you will be easily mastered by all who insult you. This is the reason why both in public and private affairs, many things occur contrary to our expectation, because we have not been diligent about spiritual things in the first place, and secondarily about the secular, but have inverted the order. For this reason also the proper sequence and right arrangement of things has been upset, and all our affairs are full of much confusion. Can you imagine what distress and grief I suffer when I observe, that if a public holy day and festival is at hand there is a concourse of all the inhabitants of the city, although there is no one to summon them; but when the holy day and festival are past, even if we should crack our voice by continuing to call over in my mind I have groaned heavily, and said to myself: What is the use of exhortation or advice, when you do everything merely by the force of habit, and do not become more zealous in consequence of my teaching? For whereas in the festivals you need no exhortation from me, but, when they are past you profit nothing by my teaching, do you not show that my discourse, so far as you are concerned, is superfluous?

4. Perhaps many of those who hear these things are grieved. But such is not the sentiment of the indolent: else they would put away their carelessness, like ourselves, who are daily anxious about your affairs. And what gain do you make by your secular transactions in proportion to the damage you sustain? It is impossible to depart from any other assembly, or gathering, in the possession of so much gain as you receive from the time spent here, whether it be the law court, or council-chamber, or even the palace itself. For we do not commit the administration of nations or cities nor the command of armies to those who enter here, but another kind of government more dignified than that of the empire itself; or rather we do not ourselves commit it, but the grace of the spirit. What then is the government, more dignified than that of the empire, which they who enter here receive? They are trained to master untoward passions, to rule wicked lusts, to command anger, to regulate ill-will, to subdue vainglory. The emperor, seated on the imperial throne, and wearing his diadem, is not so dignified as the man who has elevated his own inward right reason to the throne of government over base passions, and by his dominion over them has bound as it were a glorious diadem upon his brow. For what profit is there, pray, in purple, and raiment wrought with gold, and a jeweled crown, when the soul is in captivity to the passions? What gain is there in outward freedom when the ruling element within us is reduced to a state of disgraceful and pitiable servitude. For just as when a fever penetrates deep, and inflames all the inward parts, there is no benefit to be got from the outward surface of the body, although it is not affected in the same way: even so when our soul is violently carried away by the passion within, no outward government, not even the imperial throne, is of any profit, since reason is deposed from the throne of empire by the violent usurpation of the passions, and bows and trembles beneath their insurrectionary movements. Now to prevent this taking place prophets and apostles concur on all sides in helping us, repressing our passions, and expelling all the

ferocity of the irrational element within us, and committing a mode of government to us far more dignified than the empire. This is why I said that they who deprive themselves of this care receive a blow in the vital parts, sustaining greater damage than can be inflicted from any other quarter inasmuch as they who come here get greater gain than they could derive from any other source: even as Scripture has declared. The law said, "You shall not appear before the Lord empty"; that is, enter not into the temple without sacrifices. Now if it is not right to go into the house of God without sacrifices, much more ought we to enter the assembly accompanied by our brethren: for this sacrifice and offering is better than that, when you bring a soul with you into the Church. Do you not see doves which have been trained, how they hunt for others when they are let out? Let us also do this. For what kind of excuse shall we have, if irrational creatures are able to hunt for an animal of their own species, while we who have been honored with reason and so much wisdom neglect this kind of pursuit? I exhorted you in my former discourse with these words: "Go, each of you to the houses of your neighbors, wait for them to come out, lay hold of them, and conduct them to their common mother: and imitate those who are mad upon theatre going, who diligently arrange to meet each other and so wait at early dawn to see that iniquitous spectacle." Yet I have not effected anything by this exhortation. Therefore I speak again and shall not cease speaking, until I have persuaded you. Hearing profits nothing unless it is accompanied by practice. It makes our punishment heavier, if we continually hear the same things and do none of the things which are spoken. That the chastisement will be heavier, hear that they have "no cloak for their sin." And the Apostle says, "For not the hearers of the law shall be justified." These things he says to the hearers; but when he wishes to instruct the speaker also, that even he will not gain anything from his teaching unless his behavior is in close correspondence with his doctrine, and his manner of life is in harmony with his speech, hear how the Apostle and the prophet address themselves to him: for the latter says, "But to the sinner said God, why do you preach my laws and take my covenant in your mouth, whereas you have hated instruction?" And the Apostle, addressing himself to these same again who thought great things of their teaching, speaks in this way: "You are confident that you are a leader of the blind, a light of those who are in darkness, an instructor of the foolish, a teacher of babes: you therefore that teaches another teaches you not yourself?" Inasmuch then as it could neither profit me the speaker to speak, nor you the hearers to hear, unless we comply with the things which are spoken, but rather would increase our condemnation, let us not limit the display of our zeal to hearing only, but let us observe what is said, in our deeds. For it is indeed a good thing to spend time continually in hearing the divine oracles: but this good thing becomes useless when the benefit to be derived from hearing is not linked with it.

Therefore that you may not assemble here in vain I shall not cease beseeching you with all earnestness, as I have often besought you before, "Bring your brethren to us, exhort the wanderers, counsel them not by word only but also by deed." This is the more powerful teaching: that which comes through our manners and behavior. Even if you do not utter a word, but yet, after you have gone out of this assembly, by your actions, and your look, and your voice and all the rest of your demeanor you exhibit to the men who have been left behind the gain which you have brought away with you, this is sufficient for exhortation and advice. For we ought to go out from this place as it were from some sacred shrine, as men who have descended from heaven itself, who have become sedate, and philosophical, who do and say everything in proper measure: and when a wife sees her husband returning from the assembly, and a father his son, and a friend his friend, and an enemy his enemy, let them all receive and they perceive that you have become milder, more philosophical, more devout. Consider what privileges you enjoy who have been initiated into the mysteries, with what company you offer up that mystic hymn, with what company you cry aloud the hymn "Holy, holy, holy," are ranked as a citizen of the commonwealth above, that you have been enrolled in the choir of Angels, that you have conversed with the Lord, that you have been in the company of Christ. If we regulate ourselves in this way we shall not need to say anything, when we go out to those who are left behind: but from our advantage they will perceive their own loss and will hasten hither, so as to enjoy the same benefits themselves. For when, merely by the use of their senses, they see the beauty of your soul shining forth, even if they are the most stupid of men, they will become enamored of your goodly appearance. For if corporeal beauty excites those who behold it, much more will symmetry of soul be able to move the spectator, and stimulate him to equal zeal. Let us then adorn our inward man, and let us be mindful of the things which are said here. When we go out: for there especially is it a proper time to remember them; and just as an athlete displays in the lists the things which he has learned in the training school: even so ought we to display in our transactions in the world without the things which we have heard here.

NPNF 1.9, ed. Philip Schaff. Reprint, Peabody, MA: Hendrickson, 1994.

John Chrysostom of Constantinople (347–407)

Homily 24 on Acts

In this selection from his sermon on Acts 10:44–46, John addressed the question of the virtue of the church. The church's health was not determined by the number of those who attended worship, but their own "proved worth." "Better is one person that does the will of God than ten thousand who are transgressors." Chrysostom illustrates this by pointing out that one would prefer to have a small amount of fresh food than a large amount of diseased food. Moreover, those outside the church would not be impressed with large numbers of worshippers, but with worshippers whose lives reflected their faith.

Consequently, he instructed those in attendance to consider the worth of their worship. They sang hymns, he says, in the presence of angels. The assembly gathered in the presence of God, and should not be like a theater. Reverence was more important than revelry. Because right living was more important than merely attending the gathering of the community, believers should be prepared to rebuke the misbehavior of others for the sake of the church's purity.

Now is the trying persecution, both in this regard, and especially if it is not even thought to be persecution at all. For this persecution has also this evil in it, that being war, it is thought to be peace, so that we do not even arm ourselves against it, so that we do not even rise: no one fears, no one trembles. But if you do not believe me, ask the heathen, the persecutors, at what time was the conduct of the Christians more strict, at what time were they all more proved? Few indeed had they then become in number, but rich in virtue. For say, what profit is it, that there should be hay in plenty, when there might be precious tones? The amount consists not in the sum of numbers, but in the proved worth. Elias was one: yet the whole world was not worth so much as he. And yet the world consists of myriads: but they are no myriads, when they do not even come up to that one. "Better is one that does the will of God, than ten thousand who are transgressors": for the ten thousand have not yet reached to the one. "Desire not a multitude of unprofitable children." Such bring more blasphemy against God, than if they were not Christians. What need have I of a multitude? It is only more food for the fire. This one might see even in the body, that better is moderate food with health, than a fatted calf with damage. This is more food than the other: this is food, but that is disease. This too one may see in war: that better are ten expert and brave men, than ten thousand of no experience. These latter, besides that they do no work, hinder also those that do work. The same too one may see to be the case in a ship, viz. that better are two experienced mariners, than ever so great a number of unskillful ones: for these will sink the ship. These things I say, not as looking with an evil eye upon your numbers, but wishing that all of you should be approved men, and not trust in your numbers. Many more in number are they who go down into hell: but greater than it is the Kingdom, however few it contain. As the sand of the sea was the multitude of the people of Israel yet one man saved them. Moses was but one, and yet he availed more than they all: Joshua was one and he was enabled to do more than the six hundred thousand. Let us not make this our study merely, that the people may be many, but rather, that they may be excellent; when this shall have been effected, then will that other follow also. No one wishes at the outset to make a spacious house, but he first makes it strong and sure, then spacious: no one lays the foundations so that he may be laughed at. Let us first aim at this, and then at the other. Where this is, that also will be easy: but where this is not, the other, though it be, is to no profit. For if there be those who are able to shine in the Church, there will soon be also numbers: but where these are not, the numbers will never be good for anything. How many, suppose you, may there be in our city who are likely to be saved? It is disagreeable, what I am going to say, but I will say it nevertheless. Among all these myriads, there are not to be found one hundred likely to be saved: nay, even as to these, I question it. For think, what wickedness there is in the young, how supine are the aged! No one makes it his duty to look after his own boy, none is moved by anything to be seen in his elder, to be emulous of imitating such an one. The patterns are defaced, and therefore it is that neither do the young become admirable in conduct. Tell not me, "We are a goodly multitude": this is the speech of men who talk without thought or feeling. In the concerns of men indeed, this might be said with some show of reason: but where God is concerned—to say this with regard to him—as having need of us, can never be allowed. No, let me tell you, even in the former case, this is a senseless speech. Listen. A person that has a great number of domestics, if they be a corrupt set what a wretched time will he have of it! For him who has none, the hardship, it seems, amounts to this, that he is not waited on: but where a person has bad servants, the evil is, that he is ruining himself withal, and the damage is greater the more there are of them. For it is far worse than having to be one's own servant, to have to fight with others, and take up a continual warfare. These things I say, that none may admire the Church because of its numbers, but that we may study to make the multitude proof-worthy; that each may be earnest for his own share of the duty—not for his friends only, nor his kindred as I am always saying, nor for his neighbors, but that he may attract the strangers also. For example, prayer is going on; there they lie on bended knees, all the young, stupidly unconcerned, yes, and old too; filthy nuisances rather than young men; giggling, laughing outright, talking—for I have heard even this going on—and jeering one another as they lie along on their knees: and there stand you, young man or elder: rebuke them, if you see them behaving in this way: if any will not refrain, chide him more severely: call the deacon, threaten, do what is in your power to do: and if he dare do anything to you, assuredly you shall have all to help you. For who is so irrational, as, when he sees you chiding for such conduct, and them chidden not to take your part? Depart, having received your reward from the Prayer. In a master's house, we count those his best-disposed servants, who cannot bear to see any part of his furniture in disorder. Answer me; if at home you should see the silver plate lie tossed out of doors, though it is not your business, you will pick it up and bring it into the house: if you see a garment flung out of its place, though you have not the care of it, though you be at enmity with him whose business it is, yet, out of good-will to the master, will you not put it right? So it is in the present case. These are part of the furniture: if you see them lying about in disorder, put them to rights: apply to me, I do not refuse the trouble: inform me, make the offender known to me: it is not possible for me to see all: excuse me in this. See, what wickedness overspreads the whole world! Said I without reason that we are no better than so much hay disorderly as a troubled sea? I am not talking of those young people, that they behave in this way; what I complain of is that such a sleepy indifference possesses those who come in here, that they do not even correct this misbehavior. Again I see others stand talking while Prayer is going on; while the more consistent of them do this not only during the Prayer, but even when the Priest is giving the Benediction. O, horror! When shall there be salvation? When shall it be possible for us to propitiate God? Soldiers go to their diversion, and you shall see them, all keeping time in the dance, and nothing done negligently, but, just as in embroidery and painting, from the well-ordered arrangement in each individual part of the composition, there results at once an exceeding harmony and good keeping, so it is here: we have one shield, one head, all of us in common. And if but some casual point be deranged by negligence, the whole is deranged and is spoilt, and the good order of the many is defeated by the disorder of the one part. And, fearful indeed to think of, here you come, not to a diversion, not to act in a dance, and yet you stand disorderly. Know you not that you are standing in company with angels? With them you chant, with them sing hymns, and do you stand laughing? Is it not wonderful that a thunderbolt is not launched not only at those who behave this way, but at us? For such behavior might well be visited with the thunderbolt. The Emperor is present, is reviewing the army: and do you, even with his eyes upon you, stand laughing, and endure to see another laughing? How long are we to go on chiding, how long complaining? Ought not such to be treated as very pests and nuisances; as abandoned, worthless reprobates, fraught with innumerable acts of mischief, to be driven away from the Church? When will these forbear laughing, who laugh in the hour of the dread Mystery? When refrain from their trifling, who talk at the instant of the Benediction? Have they no sense of shame before those who are present? Have they no fear of God? Are our own idle thoughts not enough for us, is it not enough that in our prayers we rove here and there, but laughter also must intrude, and bursts of merriment? Is it a theatrical amusement, what is done here? Aye, but, I think, it is the theatres that do this: to the theatres we owe it that the most of you so refuse to be curbed by us, and to be reformed. What we build up here, is thrown down there: and not only so, but the hearers themselves cannot help being filled with other filthinesses besides: so that the case is just the same as if one should want to clean out a place with a fountain above it discharging mire; for however much you may clean out, more runs in. So it is here. For when we clean people out, as they come here from the theatres with their filthiness, thither they go again, and take in a larger stock of filthiness, as if they lived for the purpose of only giving us trouble, and then come back to us, laden with ordure, in their manners, in their movements, in their words, in their laughter, in their idleness. Then once more we begin shoveling it out afresh, as if we had to do this only on purpose that, having sent them away clean, we may again see them clogging themselves with filth. Therefore I solemnly protest to you, the sound members, that this will be to you judgment and condemnation, and I give you over to God from this time forth, if any having seen a person behaving disorderly, if any having seen any person talking, especially in that part of the worship service, shall not inform against him, not bring him round to a better behavior. To do this is better than prayer. Leave your prayer and rebuke him, that you may both do him good, and get profit yourself, and so we may be enabled all to be saved and to attain unto the Kingdom of Heaven, through the grace and mercy of our Lord Jesus Christ, with Whom to the Father and the Holy Spirit together be glory, dominion, honor, now and ever, and world without end. Amen.

NPNF 1.11, ed. Philip Schaff. Reprint, Peabody, MA: Hendrickson, 1994.

John Chrysostom of Constantinople (347–407)
Homily 29 on Acts

In this passage, John challenges the attitude that church attendance was simply a duty to be performed. The community was not considered healthy simply because it owned property and gathered together for worship. "Who has become a better person by attending daily service for a month?" he asks. Attendance at church did not necessarily indicate a proper condition. Rather, one was to desire the changed life of those who attended worship.

For the Church indeed is in very evil case, although you think her affairs to be in peace. For the mischief of it is, that while we labor under so many evils, we do not even know that we have any. "What are you saying? We are in possession of our Churches, our Church property, and all the rest, the services are held, the congregation comes to Church every day." True, but one is not to judge of the state of a Church from these things. From what then? Whether there be piety, whether we return home with profit each day, whether reaping some fruit, be it much or little, whether we do it not merely of routine and for the formal performance of a duty. Who has become a better man by attending daily service for a whole month? That is the point: otherwise the very thing which seems to bespeak a flourishing condition of the Church, does in fact bespeak an ill condition, when all this is done, and nothing comes of it. Would to God that were all, that nothing comes of it: but indeed, as things are, it turns out even for the worse. What fruit do you get from your services? Surely if you were getting any profit by them, you ought to have been long leading the life of true wisdom, with so many Prophets twice in every week discoursing to you, so many Apostles, and Evangelists, all setting forth the doctrines of salvation, and placing before you with much exactness that which can form the character aright. The soldier by going to his drill, becomes more perfect in his tactics: the wrestler by frequenting the gymnastic ground becomes more skillful in wrestling: the physician by attending on his teacher becomes more accurate, and knows more, and learns more: and you, what have you gained? I speak not to those who have been members of the Church only a year, but to those who from their earliest age have been attending the services. Do you think that to be religious is to be constant in Church-going? This is nothing unless we reap some fruit for ourselves: if from the gathering together in Church we do not gather something for ourselves, it were better to remain at home. For our forefathers built the Churches for us, not just to bring us together from our private houses and show us one to another: since this could have been done also in a marketplace, and in baths, and in a public procession, but to bring together learners and teachers, and make the one better by means of the other. With us it has all become mere customary routine, and formal discharge of a duty: a thing we are used to; that is all. Easter comes, and then great the stir, great the hubbub, and crowding of—I had rather not call them human beings, for their behavior is not commonly human. Easter goes, the tumult abates, but then the quiet which succeeds is again fruitless of good. "Vigils, and holy hymn-singing." And what is got by these? Nay, it is all the worse. Many do so merely out of vanity. Think how sick at heart it must make me, to see it all like so much water poured into a cask with holes in it! But you will assuredly say to me, we know the Scriptures. And what of that? If you exemplify the Scriptures by your works, that is the gain, that the profit. The Church is a dyer's vat: if time after time perpetually you go hence without receiving any dye, what is the use of coming here continually? Why, the mischief is all the greater. Who of you has added anything to the customary practices he received from his fathers? For example, someone has a custom of observing the memorial of his mother, or his wife, or his child: this he does whether he is told or whether he is not told by us, drawn to it by force of habit and conscience. Does this displease you, you ask? God forbid: on the contrary, I am glad of it with all my heart: only, I would wish that he had gained some fruit also from our discoursing, and that the effect which habit has, were also the effect as regards us, your teachers, the introduction of another habit. Else why do I weary myself in vain, and talk uselessly, if you are to remain in the same state, if the Church services work no good in you? Nay, you will say, we pray. And what of that? "Not every one that says unto me, Lord, Lord, shall enter into the Kingdom of heaven; but he that does the will of my Father which is in heaven." Many a time have I determined to hold my peace, seeing no benefit accruing to you from my words; or perhaps there does accrue some, but I, through insatiableness and strong desire, am affected in the same way as those that are mad after riches. For just as they, however much they may get, think they have nothing; so I, because I ardently desire your salvation, until I see you to have made good progress, think nothing done, because of my exceeding eager desire that you should arrive at the very summit. I would that this were the case, and that my eagerness were in fault, not your sloth: but I fear I conjecture but too rightly. For you need to be persuaded, that if any benefit had arisen in all this length of time, would have stopped speaking. In such case, there were no need to you of words, since both in those already spoken there had been enough said for you, and you would be yourselves able to correct others. But the fact, that there is still a necessity of our discoursing to you, only shows, that matters with you are not in a state of high perfection. Then what would we have to be brought about? For one must not merely find fault. I beseech and entreat you not to think it enough to have invaded the Church, but that you also withdraw hence, having taken somewhat, some medicine, for the curing of your own maladies: and, if not from us, at any rate from the Scriptures, you have the remedies suitable for each. For instance, is any passionate? Let him attend to the Scripture readings, and he will of a surety find such either in history or exhortation.

NPNF 1.11, ed. Philip Schaff. Reprint, Peabody, MA: Hendrickson, 1994.

ADDITIONAL READINGS

Burtchaell, J. T. From Synagogue to Church: Public Services and Offices in the Earliest Christian Communities. Cambridge: Cambridge University Press, 1992.
Casel, O. The Mystery of Christian Worship. Westminster, MD: Newman, 1962.
Dix, G. The Shape of the Liturgy. Westminster, London: Dacre, 1945.
Ferguson, E., ed. Worship in Early Christianity, Studies in Early Christianity, vol. 15. New York: Garland, 1993.

CHAPTER 3

Instructing the Community

Proclamation in the Early Church

அ

In the previous chapter we noticed that a central element of early Christian worship was the reading and exposition of the Scriptures. These sermons, as they were called, were the means by which pastors of churches instructed their congregations in what to believe about God and how to live lives that reflected a Christian commitment. Christians believed that God had spoken through the Bible, and it was the role of the preacher to explain its meaning to them. This didactic device had its background in similar Jewish practices.

Preaching was done in a number of contexts. While the regular worship service was the primary occasion for instruction, there were also other organized times of teaching for the congregation. The church would offer classes exclusively for the catechumens in which they would receive basic tutelage in the faith. There would be messages delivered at various times for interested nonbelievers to learn about Christianity, particularly in a place such as Alexandria. Sometimes preachers would share their message in the public square, as can be seen in Acts 17, when the Apostle Paul preached at Mars Hill.

Christian sermons were regularly transcribed in order to preserve the message for others. Members who were not present at a particular service could review the sermon later. The preacher could deliver the message again, either in the same congregation or somewhere else. Sermons intended for particular groups, such as the catechumens, could be used subsequently without entirely new preparations. As we will see in Augustine, it was routine for preachers to deliver someone else's message, made possible by a written manuscript. These homilies were often circulated with other significant writings, such as was the case with *Second Clement*, a second-century sermon.

Those who gave sermons were generally the elders of churches. These pastors were authorized to preach by their ordination, or selection by the congregation to be leaders of the community.[1] They were chosen from within the church because they had demonstrated exemplary Christian living and an ability to teach others. There was no official body responsible for overseeing the affairs of all the churches, as there would be later. Gradually, as the bishop became the administrator of a number of churches, the role of sanctioning pastors of particular congregations became his.

Often, especially in earlier times, pastors would welcome itinerant preachers to share with the congregation. However, as the *Didache* admonished,[2] great care was needed to ensure that the visiting minister would not teach something contrary to right Christian faith. These traveling preachers would often share the message of the Gospel in places where no Christian community existed. Their purpose was to seek converts who would constitute a church.[3] With the spread of Christianity, and its subsequent acceptance throughout the Roman Empire, the need for itinerant ministers greatly diminished.

Augustine of Hippo and John Chrysostom of Constantinople feature prominently in this chapter because they are two of the best exemplars of the kinds of issues of concern for preachers in early Christianity. Of particular interest are their respective opinions regarding the role of rhetorical tools in the delivery of sermons. Augustine encouraged preachers to develop a style of delivery that would be pleasant to hear in order to attract the attention of listeners. He argued that a hearer would more likely hear the message if it were entertaining. However, he cautioned against diminishing the content of the sermon for the sake of entertainment. Chrysostom, on the other hand, dissuaded young preachers from employing oratorical devices that might interfere with the audience's ability to hear significant instruction or exhortation. The congregation would be happy, he argued, but not healthy. Additionally, the preacher might become more interested in delivering messages that were popular or appealing to the people than were expositions that were concerned with their spiritual well-being. These differing views of preaching styles continue to be debated within Christianity.

Second Clement (Early Second Century)

This is the oldest remaining sermon outside the New Testament, delivered early in the second century. A written copy of the message was circulated along with Clement of Rome's *First Letter to the Corinthians,* otherwise known as *First Clement,* sometime before the fourth century. This association gives the homily its name. However, it is now generally agreed that the preacher of this message was not Clement. Though the author is unknown, the title is still used. Nothing definite is known about its origin or original context, though one might speculate that because of its association with Clement's *Letter* it was possibly delivered either in Rome or Corinth.

The preacher exhorted his listeners to focus their thinking on the coming kingdom of the Lord: Christ would one day return to earth bringing with him reward for his faithful followers and judgment for those who did not obey him. Christians were inspired to endure what hardships they faced with optimism that one day they would live in a better world, in which their suffering would be relieved and they would enjoy eternal life. Grieving on earth would one day give way to rejoicing in heaven. The preacher instructed them that they would one day be resurrected from the dead just as their Lord had been.

In addition, the message warned its hearers of the judgment Christ would administer upon his return. Fear of punishment was to encourage the Christians to live according to the commands and instructions of God. One day, the community was instructed, every person would give account for his or her actions. Those who had obeyed God would receive eternal life. Those who had not obeyed would receive eternal punishment.

This early Greek sermon is important because it serves as the earliest example of Christian preaching from the period after the Apostles. It illustrates the common emphasis on the future. Believers who had little hope for earthly wealth or prominence find hope in the expectation of the return of Christ. The circulation of this sermon with Clement of Rome's letter to the Corinthian church indicates the importance of this theme even long after the initial presentation of the sermon.

Brothers and sisters, it is fitting that you should think of Jesus Christ as of God, that is, as the Judge of the living and the dead. And it does not become us to think lightly of our salvation; for if we think little of him, we shall also hope but to obtain little from him. And those of us who hear carelessly of

these things, as if they were of small importance, commit sin, not knowing from where we have been called, and by whom, and to what place, and how much Jesus Christ submitted to suffer for our sakes. What return, then, shall we make to him, or what fruit that shall be worthy of that which he has given to us? For, indeed, how great are the benefits that we owe to him! He has graciously given us light; as a Father, he has called us sons; he has saved us when we were ready to perish. What praise, then, shall we give to him, or what return shall we make for the things that we have received? We were deficient in understanding, worshipping stones and wood, and gold, and silver, and brass, the works of men's hands; and our whole life was nothing else than death. Involved in blindness, and with such darkness before our eyes, we have received sight, and through his will have laid aside that cloud by which we were enveloped. For he had compassion on us, and mercifully saved us, observing the many errors in which we were entangled, as well as the destruction to which we were exposed, and that we had no hope of salvation except it came to us from him. For he called us when we were not, and willed that out of nothing we should attain a real existence. . . .

Since he has displayed so great mercy towards us, and especially in this respect, that we who are living should not offer sacrifices to gods that are dead, or pay them worship, but should attain through him to the knowledge of the true Father, how will we show that we do indeed know him, but by not denying him through whom this knowledge has been attained? For he himself declares, "Whosoever shall confess me before men, him will I confess before my Father." This, then, is our reward if we shall confess him by whom we have been saved. But in what way shall we confess him? By doing what he says, and not transgressing his commandments, and by honoring him not with our lips only, but with all our heart and our entire mind. For he says in Isaiah, "These people honor me with their lips, but their hearts are far from me." . . .

Therefore, brethren, leaving willingly our sojourn in this present world, let us do the will of him that called us, and not fear to depart out of this world. For the Lord said, "You shall be as lambs in the midst of wolves." And Peter answered and said unto him, "What, then, if the wolves shall tear in pieces the lambs?" Jesus said unto Peter, "The lambs have no cause after they are dead to fear the wolves; and in like manner, fear not you them that kill you, and can do nothing more unto you; but fear him who, after you are dead, has power over both soul and body to cast them into hell-fire." And consider, brethren, that the sojourning in the flesh in this world is but brief and transient, but the promise of Christ is great and wonderful, even the rest of the kingdom to come, and of life everlasting. By what course of conduct, then, shall we attain these things, but by leading a holy and righteous life, and by deeming these worldly things as not belonging to us, and not fixing our desires upon them? For if we desire to possess them, we fall away from the path of righteousness. . . .

As long, therefore, as we are upon earth, let us practice repentance, for we are as clay in the hand of the artist. For as the potter, if he make a vessel, and it be distorted or broken in his hands, fashions it over again; but if he have before this cast it into the furnace of fire, can no longer find any help for it: so let us also, while we are in this world, repent with our whole heart of the evil deeds we have done in the flesh, that we may be saved by the Lord, while we have yet an opportunity of repentance. For after we have gone out of the world, no further power of confessing or repenting will there belong to us. Therefore, brethren, by doing the will of the Father, and keeping the flesh holy, and observing the commandments of the Lord, we shall obtain eternal life. For the Lord said in the Gospel, "If you have not kept that which was small, who will commit to you the great? For I say unto you, that he that is faithful in that which is least, is faithful also in much." This, then, is what he means: "Keep the flesh holy and the seal undefiled, that you may receive eternal life."

And let no one of you say that this very flesh shall not be judged, nor rise again. Consider in what state you were saved, in what you received sight, if not while you were in this flesh. We must therefore preserve the flesh as the temple of God. For as you were called in the flesh, you shall also come to be judged in the flesh. As Christ the Lord who saved us, though he was first a Spirit became flesh, and thus called us, so shall we also receive the reward in this flesh. Let us therefore love one another, that we may all attain to the kingdom of God. While we have an opportunity of being healed, let us yield ourselves to God that heals us, and give to him recompense. Of what sort? Repentance out of a sincere heart; for he knows all things beforehand, and is acquainted with what is in our hearts. Let us therefore give him praise, not with the mouth only, but also with the heart, that he may accept us as sons. For the Lord has said, "Those are my brethren who do the will of my Father." . . .

Let us expect, therefore, hour by hour, the kingdom of God in love and righteousness, since we know not the day of the appearing of God. For the Lord himself, being asked by one when his kingdom would come, replied,

"When two shall be one, that which is without as that which is within, and the male with the female, neither male nor female." Now, two are one when we speak the truth one to another, and there is unfeigned one soul in two bodies. And "that which is without as" that which is within means this: he calls the soul "that which is within," and the body "that which is without." As, then, your body is visible to sight, so also let your soul be manifest by good works. And "the male, with the female, neither male nor female," this he said, that brother seeing sister may have no thought concerning her as female, and that she may have no thought concerning him as male. "If you do these things, said he, "the kingdom of my Father shall come." . . .

So, then, brethren, having received no small occasion to repent, while we have opportunity, let us turn to God who called us, while yet we have One to receive us. For if we renounce these indulgences and conquer the soul by not fulfilling its wicked desires, we shall be partakers of the mercy of Jesus. Know you that the day of judgment draws near like a burning oven, and certain of the heavens and all the earth will melt, like lead melting in fire; and then will appear the hidden and manifest deeds of men. Good deeds are as repentance from sin; better is fasting than prayer, and good works than both; "charity covers a multitude of sins," and prayer out of a good conscience delivers from death. Blessed is every one that shall be found complete in these; for good works lighten the burden of sin.

Let us, then, repent with our whole heart, that no one of us may perish amiss. For if we have commands and engage in withdrawing from idols and instructing others, how much more ought a soul already knowing God not to perish. Rendering, therefore, mutual help, let us raise the weak also in that which is good, that all of us may be saved and convert one another and admonish. And not only now let us seem to believe and give heed, when we are admonished by the elders; but also when we take our departure home, let us remember the commandments of the Lord, and not be allured back by worldly lusts, but let us often and often draw near and try to make progress in the Lord's commands, that we all having the same mind may be gathered together for life. For the Lord said, "I come to gather all nations and tongues." This means the day of his appearing, when he will come and redeem us—each one according to his works. And the unbelievers will see his glory and might, and, when they see the empire of the world in Jesus, they will be surprised, saying, "Woe to us, because you were, and we knew not and believed not and obeyed not the elders who show us plainly of our salvation." And "their worm shall not die, neither shall their fire be quenched; and they shall be a spectacle unto all flesh." It is of the great Day of Judgment he speaks, when they shall see those among us who were guilty of ungodliness and erred in their estimate of the commands of Jesus Christ. The righteous, having succeeded both in enduring the trials and hating the indulgences of the soul, whenever they witness how those who have swerved and denied Jesus by words or deeds are punished with grievous torments in fire unquenchable, will give glory to their God and say, "There will be hope for him who has served God with his whole heart." . . .

So then, brothers and sisters, after the God of truth I address to you an appeal that you may give heed to the words written, that you may save both yourselves and him who reads an address in your midst. For as a reward I ask of you repentance with the whole heart, while you bestow upon yourselves salvation and life. For by so doing we shall set a mark for all the young who wish to be diligent in godliness and the goodness of God. And let not us, in our folly, feel displeasure and indignation, whenever any one admonishes us and turns us from unrighteousness to righteousness. For there are some wicked deeds which we commit, and know it not, because of the double-mindedness and unbelief present in our breasts, and our understanding is darkened by vain desires. Let us, therefore, work righteousness, that we may be saved to the end. Blessed are they who obey these commandments, even if for a brief space they suffer in this world, and they will gather the imperishable fruit of the resurrection. Let not the godly person, therefore, grieve; if for the present he suffer affliction, blessed is the time that awaits him there; rising up to life again with the fathers he will rejoice for ever without a grief.

ANF 8, ed. A. Cleveland Coxe. Reprint, Peabody, MA: Hendrickson, 1994.

Cyril of Jerusalem (315–386)
Prologue to Catechetical Lectures

Cyril delivered these lectures early in his tenure as pastor of the church at Jerusalem to the catechumens, or those preparing for baptism and initiation into the community of faith. In the prologue to these messages, he explained their importance: they prepared believers for their warfare against false teaching. He contrasted the lectures he would deliver with regular sermons preached in worship. The former provided the foundation for what would be learned in the latter. While one could miss a sermon one week and remain able to understand the next week's message, the *Catechetical Lectures* built on one another in succession, and served as the foundation for the future homilies one would hear. This selection affords a glimpse not only into Cyril's immediate instruction to candidates for baptism but also into the continued importance of preaching for the life of the Christian community.

10. Attend closely to the teaching, and though we should prolong our discourse, let not your mind be wearied out. For you are receiving armor against adverse power. . . . You have many enemies; take many darts, for you have many to hurl them at: and you have need to learn how to strike down the Greek, how to contend against heretic, against Jew and Samaritan. And the armor is ready, and most ready the sword of the Spirit: but you also must stretch forth your right hand with good resolution, that you may war the Lord's warfare, and overcome adverse powers, and become invincible against every heretical attempt.

11. Let me give you this charge also. Study our teachings and keep them forever. Think not that they are the ordinary homilies; for though they also are good and trustworthy, yet if we should neglect them today we may study them tomorrow. But if the teaching concerning baptism delivered in a consecutive course is neglected today, when shall it be made right? Suppose it is the season for planting trees: if we do not dig, and dig deep, when else can that be planted rightly which has once been planted improperly? Suppose, I ask, that the teaching is a kind of building: if we do not bind the house together by regular bonds in the building, lest some gap be found, and the building become unsound, even our former labor is of no use. But stone must follow stone by course, and corner match with corner, and by our smoothing off inequalities the building must thus rise evenly. In like manner we are bringing to you stones, as it were, of knowledge. You must hear concerning the living God, you must hear of Judgment, must hear of Christ, and of the Resurrection. And many things there are to be discussed in succession, which though now dropped one by one are afterwards to be presented in harmonious connection. But unless you fit them together in the one whole, and remember what is first, and what is second, the builder may build, but you will find the building unsound.

NPNF 2.7, ed. W. Sanday. Reprint, Peabody, MA: Hendrickson, 1994.

John Chrysostom of Constantinople (347–407)

On the Priesthood

This treatise of John's instructed young pastors to examine diligently their personal lives and their ministries. He intended it to explain the requirements of ministry and the minister, both regarding character and responsibilities. John focused his attention on the pastor as preacher. He taught two essential characteristics of the effective preacher: ambivalence concerning one's popularity with the congregation and the skill of preaching well.

A preacher was not to desire the applause of his listeners. Rather, he was to long for the conformation of their lives to his message. Likewise, John called on ministers to disregard inappropriate criticism and slander. If one were consumed with seeking merely to please the audience, truth would give way to pandering. Humility should characterize the preacher. His emphasis on leading the people to listen for their profit rather than their pleasure can be contrasted with Augustine's instruction in this regard (see below).

Chrysostom also exhorted his readers to prepare laboriously for the task of explaining the Scriptures to the community. The pastor's task was to instruct members in the way of Christ to prevent their demise. The job required skill in reading and interpreting the Bible, and it required hard work and perseverance.

Book Four

9. But when a dispute arises concerning matters of doctrine, and all take their weapons from the same Scriptures, of what weight will any one's life be able to prove? What then will be the good of his many austerities, when after such painful exercises, any one from the pastor's great lack of skill in argument fall into heresy, and be cut off from the body of the Church, a misfortune which I have myself seen many suffering. Of what profit then will his patience be to him? None; no more than there will be in a sound faith if the life is corrupt. Therefore, for this reason more than for all others, it concerns him whose office it is to teach others, to be experienced in disputations of this kind. For though he himself stands safely, and is unhurt by the gainsayers, yet the simple multitude under his direction, when they see their leader defeated, and without any answer for the gainsayers, will be apt to lay the blame of his

discomfiture not on his own weakness, but on the doctrines themselves, as though they were faulty; and so by reason of the inexperience of one, great numbers are brought to extreme ruin; for though they do not entirely go over to the adversary, yet they are forced to doubt about matters in which formerly they firmly believed, and those whom they used to approach with unswerving confidence, they are unable to hold to any longer steadfastly, but in consequence of their leader's defeat, so great a storm settles down upon their souls, that the mischief ends in their shipwreck altogether. But how dire is the destruction, and how terrible the fire which such a leader brings upon his own wretched head for every soul which is thus lost, you will not need to learn from me, as you know all this perfectly. Is this then pride, is this vainglory in me, to be unwilling to be the cause of the destruction of so many souls? and of procuring for myself greater punishment in the world to come, than that which now awaits me there? Who would say so? Surely no one, unless he should wish to find fault where there is none, and to moralize over other men's calamities.

Book Five

1. We have already set forth sufficiently what great skill is required for the preacher in earnestly contending for the truth. But I have to mention one more matter beside this, which is a cause of countless dangers, though for my own part I should rather say that the thing itself is not the cause, but they who know not how to use it rightly, since it is of itself a help to salvation and to much good besides, whenever you find that earnest and good men have the management of it. What then, do I mean by this? I mean the expenditure of great labor upon the preparation of sermons to be delivered in public. For to begin with, the majority of those who are under the preachers' charge are not minded to behave towards them as towards teachers, but disdaining the part of learners, they assume instead the attitude of those who sit and look on at the public games; and just as the multitude there is separated into parties, and some attach themselves to one, and some to another, so here also men are divided, and become the partisans now of this teacher, now of that, listening to them with a view to favor or spite. And not only is there this hardship, but another quite as great. For if it has occurred to any preacher to weave into his sermons any part of other men's works, he is exposed to greater disgrace than those who steal money. Nay, often where he has not even borrowed anything from any one, but is only suspected, he has suffered the fate of a thief. And

why do I speak of the works of others when it is not permitted to him to use his own resources without variety? For the public are accustomed to listen not for profit, but for pleasure, sitting like critics of tragedies, and of musical entertainments, and that facility of speech against which we declaimed just now, in this case becomes desirable, even more than in the case of barristers, where they are obliged to contend one against the other. A preacher then should have loftiness of mind, far exceeding my own littleness of spirit, that he may correct this disorderly and unprofitable pleasure on the part of the multitude, and be able to lead them over to a more useful way of hearing, that his people may follow and yield to him, and that he may not be led away by their own humors, and this it is not possible to arrive at, except by two means: indifference to their praise, and the power of preaching well.

2. For if either of these be lacking, the remaining one becomes useless, owing to its divorce from the other, for if a preacher be indifferent to praise, and yet cannot produce the doctrine "which is with grace seasoned with salt," he becomes despised by the multitude, while he gains nothing from his own nobleness of mind; and if on the other hand he is successful as a preacher, and is overcome by the thought of applause, harm is equally done in turn, both to himself and the multitude, because in his desire for praise he is careful to speak rather with a view to please than to profit. And as he who neither lets good opinion influence him, nor is skillful in speaking, does not yield to the pleasure of the multitude, and is unable to do them any good worth mentioning, because he has nothing to say, so he who is carried away with desire for praise, though he is able to render the multitude better service, rather provides in place of this such food as will suit their taste, because he purchases thereby the tumult of acclamation. . . .

4. To what else ought he then to be indifferent? Slander and envy. Unseasonable evil speaking. However (for of course the pastor undergoes some groundless censure), it is well that he should neither fear nor tremble at excessively, nor entirely pass over; but we ought, though it happen to be false, or to be brought against us by the common herd, to try and extinguish it immediately. For nothing so magnifies both an evil and a good report as the undisciplined mob. For accustomed to hear and to speak without stopping to make inquiry, they repeat at random everything that comes in their way, without any regard to the truth of it. Therefore the pastor ought not to be unconcerned about the multitude, but straightway to nip their evil surmising in the bud; persuading his accusers, even if they are the most unreasonable of all men, and to omit nothing that is able to dispel an ill-favored

report. But if, when we do all this, they who blame us will not be persuaded, thenceforward we should give them no concern. Since if any one is too quick to be dejected by these accidents, he will not be able at any time to produce anything noble and admirable. For despondency and constant cares are mighty for destroying the powers of the mind, and for reducing it to extreme weakness. Thus then must the pastor behave towards those in his charge, as a father would behave to his very young children; and as such is not disturbed either by their insults or their blows, or their lamentations, nor even if they laugh and rejoice with us, do we take much account of it; so should we neither be puffed up by the promises of these persons nor cast down at their censure, when it comes from them unseasonably. But this is hard, my good friend; and perhaps, methinks, even impossible. For I know not whether any man ever succeeded in the effort not to be pleased when he is praised, and the man who is pleased at this is likely also to desire to enjoy it, and the man who desires to enjoy it will, of necessity, be altogether vexed and beside himself whenever he misses it. For as they who revel in being rich, when they fall into poverty are grieved, and they who have been used to live luxuriously cannot bear to live shabbily; so, too, they who long for applause, not only when they are blamed without a cause, but when they are not constantly being praised, become, as by some famine, wasted in soul, particularly when they happen themselves to have been used to praise, or if they hear others being praised. He who enters upon the trial of preaching with desires of this kind, how many annoyances and how many pangs do you think that he has? It is no more possible for the sea to be without waves than that man to be without cares and grief. . . .

6. You see, my excellent friend, that the man who is powerful in preaching has peculiar need of greater study than others; and besides study, of forbearance also greater than what is needed by all those whom I have already mentioned. For thus are many constantly springing up against him, in a vain and senseless spirit, and having no fault to find with him, but that he is generally approved of, hate him; and he must bear their bitter malice nobly, for as they are not able to hide this cursed hatred, which they so unreasonably entertain, they both revile, and censure, and slander in private, and defame in public, and the mind which has begun to be pained and exasperated, on every one of these occasions, will not escape being corrupted by grief. For they will not only revenge themselves upon him by their own acts, but will try to do so by means of others, and often having chosen some one of those who are unable to speak a word, will extol him with their praises and admire him beyond his

worth. Some do this through ignorance alone, some through ignorance and envy, in order that they may ruin the reputation of the other, not that they may prove the man to be wonderful who is not so, and the noble-minded man has not only to struggle against these, but often against the ignorance of the whole multitude; for since it is not possible that all those who come together should consist of learned men, but the chances are that the larger part of the congregation is composed of unlearned people, and that even the rest, who are clearer headed than they, fall as far short of being able to criticize sermons as the remainder again fall short of them; so that only one or two are seated there who possess this power; it follows, of necessity, that he who preaches better than others carries away less applause, and possibly goes home without being praised at all, and he must be prepared to meet such anomalies nobly, and to pardon those who commit them in ignorance, and to weep for those who acquiesce in them on account of envy as wretched and pitiable creatures, and not to consider that his powers have become less on either of these accounts. For if a man, being a pre-eminently good painter, and superior to all in his art, sees the portrait which he has drawn with great accuracy held up to ridicule, he ought not to be dejected, and to consider the picture poor, because of the judgment of the ignorant; as he would not consider the drawing that is really poor to be something wonderful and lovely, because of the astonishment of the inartistic. . . .

8. For if he be first carried away with the desire for indiscriminate praise, he will reap no advantage from his labors, or from his power in preaching, for the mind being unable to bear the senseless censures of the multitude is dispirited, and casts aside all earnestness about preaching. Therefore it is especially necessary to be trained to be indifferent to all kinds of praise. For to know how to preach is not enough for the preservation of that power, if this be not added: and if any one would examine accurately the man who is destitute of this art, he will find that he needs to be indifferent to praise no less than the other, for he will be forced to do many wrong things in placing himself under the control of popular opinion. For not having the energy to equal those who are in repute for the quality of their preaching, he will not refrain from forming ill designs against them, from envying them, and from blaming them without reason, and from many such discreditable practices, but will venture everything, even if it be needful to ruin his own soul, for the sake of bringing down their fame to the level of his own insignificance. And in addition to this, he will leave off his exertions about his work; a kind of numbness, as it were, spreading itself over his mind. For much toil, rewarded by

scanty praise, is sufficient to cast down a man who cannot despise praise, and put him into a deep lethargy, since the husbandman even when he spends time over some sorry piece of land, and is forced to till a rock, quickly desists from his work, unless he is possessed of much earnestness about the matter, or has a fear of famine impending over him. For if they who are able to speak with considerable power, need such constant exercise for the preservation of their talent, he who collects no materials at all, but is forced in the midst of his efforts to meditate; what difficulty, what confusion, what trouble will he experience, in order that he may be able at great labor to collect a few ideas! and if any of those clergy who are under his authority, and who are placed in the inferior order, be able in that position to appear to be of a better advantage than he, what a divine mind must he have, so as not to be seized with envy or cast down by despondency. For, for one to be placed in a station of higher dignity, and to be surpassed by his inferior in rank, and to bear this nobly, would not be the part of any ordinary mind, nor of such as my own, but of one as hard as adamant; and if, indeed, the man who is in greater repute be very forbearing and modest, the suffering becomes so much the more easily borne. But if he is bold and boastful and vainglorious, a daily death would be desirable for the other; he will so embitter his life, insulting him to his face, and laughing at him behind his back, wresting much of his authority from him, and wishing to be everything himself. But he is possessed of the greatest security, in all these circumstances, who has fluency in preaching, and the earnest attention of the multitude about him, and the affection of all those who are under his charge. Do you not know what a passion for sermons has burst in upon the minds of Christians now a day? and that they who practice themselves in preaching are in especial honor, not only among the heathen, but also among them of the household of the faith? How then could any one bear such disgrace as to find that all are mute when he is preaching, and think that they are oppressed, and wait for the end of the sermon, as for some release from work; while they listen to another with eagerness though he preach long, and are sorry when he is about to conclude; and almost angry when it is his purpose to be silent. If these matters seem to you to be small, and easily to be despised, it is because of your inexperience. They are truly enough to quench zeal, and to paralyze the powers of the mind, unless a man withdraw himself from all human passions, and study to frame his conduct after the pattern of those incorporeal powers, who are neither pursued by envy, nor by longing for fame, nor by any other morbid feeling. If then there be any man so constituted as to be able to subdue this wild beast, so difficult to capture, so unconquerable, so fierce; that is to say, public fame, and to cut off its many heads, or rather to forbid their growth altogether; he will easily be able to repel these many violent assaults, and to enjoy a kind of quiet haven of rest. But he who has not freed himself from this monster, involves his soul in struggles of various kinds, and perpetual agitation, and the burden both of despondency and of other passions. But why need I detail the rest of these difficulties, which no one will be able to describe, or to learn unless he has had actual experience of them.

NPNF 1.9, ed. Philip Schaff. Reprint, Peabody, MA: Hendrickson, 1994.

John Chrysostom of Constantinople (347–407)
Homily 33 on Acts

This selection expounds somewhat on the previous one. Here Chrysostom chastised preachers for thinking highly of themselves because of their ability to communicate. This pride, he indicated, had led to the fall of many other pastors. One's lifestyle was to match one's message; otherwise the congregation would accept little of the teaching. This credibility must have been a problem for those preaching to the community in the fourth century. One might expect this to be the case in Constantinople, the capital of the empire at the time. With numerous significant churches, attended by very important people, one would have been tempted to seek the approval of one's listeners. In addition, there would have been scores of highly educated orators in the city, vying for the attention of the people.

The bulk of John's sermon dealt with the people's applause. The community must have been quite vocal in response to John's preaching, and he found it to be an unwelcome disturbance. He even indicated that he had considered not allowing the congregation to applaud, after which they appear to have applauded! Such behavior, he said, belonged in the theaters. The assembly was to be a place of quiet reflection, not rambunctious entertainment.

Why do you think great things of yourself? Because you teach by words? But this is easy, to philosophize in words: teach me by your life: that is the best

teaching. Do you say that it is right to be moderate, and do you make a long speech about this thing, and play the orator, pouring forth your eloquence without a check? But "better than you is he" shall one say to you, "who teaches me this by his deeds"—for not so much are those lessons wont to be fixed in the mind which consist in words, as those which teach by things: since if you have not the deed, you not only have not profited him by your words, but have even hurt him the more: "better you were silent." Therefore? "Because the thing you propose to me is impossible: for I consider, that if you who have so much to say about it, succeed not in this, much more am I excusable." For this cause the Prophet says, "But unto the sinner said God. Why do you preach my statutes?" For this is a worse mischief, when one who teaches well in words, impugns the teaching by his deeds. This has been the cause of many evils in the Churches. Therefore pardon me, I beseech you, that my discourse dwells long on this evil affection. Many take a deal of pains to be able to stand up in public, and make a long speech: and if they get applause from the multitude, it is to them as if they gained the very kingdom of heaven: but if silence follows the close of their speech, it is worse than hell itself, the dejection that falls upon their spirits from the silence! This has turned the Churches upside down, because both of you desire not to hear a discourse calculated to lead you to compunction, but one that may delight you from the sound and composition of the words, as though you were listening to singers and minstrels: and we too act a preposterous and pitiable part in being led by your lusts, when we ought to root them out. And so it is just as if the father of a poor cold-blooded child already more delicate than it ought to be, should, although it is so feeble, give it cake and cold drink and whatever only pleases the child, and take no account of what might do it good; and then, being reproved by the physicians, should excuse himself by saying, "What can I do? I cannot bear to see the child crying." You poor, wretched creature, you betrayer! for I cannot, call such a one a father: how much better were it for you, by paining him for a short time, to restore him to health forever, than to make this short-lived pleasure the foundation of a lasting sorrow? Just such is our case, when we idly busy ourselves about beautiful expressions, and the composition and harmony of our sentences, in order that we may please, not profit: when we make it our aim to be admired, not to instruct; to delight, not prick to the heart; to be applauded and depart with praise, not to correct men's manners! Believe me, I speak not other than I feel—when as I discourse I hear myself applauded, at the moment indeed I feel it as a man (for why should I not own the truth?): I am delighted, and give way to the pleasurable feeling: but when I get home, and bethink me that those who applauded received no benefit from my discourse, but that whatever benefit they ought to have got, they lost it while applauding and praising, I am in pain, and groan, and weep, and feel as if I had spoken all in vain. I say to myself: "What profit comes to me from my labors, while the hearers do not choose to benefit by what they hear from us?" Nay, often have I thought to make a rule that should prevent all applauding, and persuade you to listen with silence and becoming orderliness. But bear with me, I beseech you, and be persuaded by me, and, if it seem good to you, let us even now establish this rule, that no hearer be permitted to applaud in the midst of any person's discourse, but if he will needs admire, let him admire in silence: there is none to prevent him: and let all his study and eager desire be set upon the receiving the things spoken.—What means that noise again? I am laying down a rule against this very thing, and you have not the forbearance even to hear me!—Many will be the good effects of this regulation: it will be a discipline of philosophy. Even the heathen philosophers—we hear of their discoursing, and nowhere do we find that noisy applause accompanied their words: we hear of the Apostles, making public speeches, and yet nowhere do the accounts add, that in the midst of their speeches the hearers interrupted the speakers with loud expressions of approbation. A great gain will this be to us. But let us establish this rule: in quiet let us all hear, and speak the whole of what we have to say. For if indeed it were the case that we departed retaining what we had heard, what I insist upon is, that even so the praise is not beneficial—but not to go too much into particulars on this point; let none tax me with rudeness—but since nothing is gained by it, nay, it is even mischievous, let us loose the hindrance, let us put a stop to the bounding, let us retrench the gamboling of the soul. Christ spoke publicly on the Mount: yet no one said aught, until he had finished his discourse. I do not rob those who wish to be applauded: on the contrary, I make them to be more admired. It is far better that one's hearer, having listened in silence, should by his memory throughout all time applaud, both at home and abroad, than that having lost all he should return home empty, not possessed of that which was the subject of his applauses. For how shall the hearer be otherwise than ridiculous? Nay, he will be deemed a flatterer, and his praises no better than irony, when he declares that the teacher spoke beautifully, but what he said, this he cannot tell. This has all the appearance of adulation. For when indeed one has been hearing minstrels and players, it is no wonder if such be the case with him, seeing he knows not how to utter the strain in the same manner: but where the matter is not an exhibition of song or of voice, but the drift and purport of thoughts and wise reflection, and it is easy for every one to tell and report what was said, how can he but deserve the accusation, who cannot tell what the matter was for which he praised the speaker? Nothing so becomes a Church as silence and good order. Noise belongs to theatres, and baths, and public processions, and market places: but where doctrines, and such doctrines, are the subject of teaching, there should be stillness, and quiet, and calm reflection, and a haven of much repose. These things I beseech and entreat: for I go about in quest of ways by which I shall be enabled to profit your souls. And no small way I take this to be: it will profit not you only, but us also. So shall we not be carried away with pride, not be tempted to love praises and honor, not be led to speak those things which delight, but those which profit: so shall we lay the whole stress of our time and diligence not upon arts of composition and beauties of expression, but upon the matter and meaning of the thoughts. Go into a painter's study, and you will observe how silent all is there. Then so ought it to be here: for here too we are employed in painting portraits, royal portraits (every one of them), none of any private man, by means of the colors of virtue—How now? Applauding again? This reform is not easily effected, but only by reason of long habit—the pencil moreover is the tongue, and the Artist the Holy Spirit. Tell me, is there any noise made during the celebration of the Mysteries? Is there any disturbance when we are baptizing or when we are doing any of the other acts? Is not all nature decked as it were with stillness and silence? Over all the face of heaven is scattered this charm of repose. On this account are we evil spoken of even among the Gentiles, as though we did all for display and ostentation? But if this is prevented, the love of the chief seats also will be extinguished. It is sufficient, if any one is enamored of praise, that he should obtain it after having been heard, when all is gathered in. Yea, I beseech you, let us establish this rule, that doing all things according to God's will, we may be found worthy of the mercy which is from him, through the grace and compassion of his only begotten Son our Lord Jesus Christ, with Whom to the Father together with the Holy Spirit be glory, dominion, honor, now and ever, world without end. Amen.

NPNF 1.11, ed. Philip Schaff. Reprint, Peabody, MA: Hendrickson, 1994.

John Chrysostom of Constantinople (347–407)
Homily 32 on the Gospel of John

This sermon reveals that the Christian community remained heavily involved in the general social life of fourth-century Constantinople, much to Chrysostom's chagrin. His purpose was to contrast the people's insatiable desire to attend the theaters, athletic events, and festivals, with their sloth in attending the times of preaching where the Scriptures were explained. It was there that wrestling against Satan took place. Knowledge of the Bible would serve to sustain the congregation, yet believers, according to John, knew more about the families of athletes than about the Christian Scriptures. He expected some of his hearers to be offended by his exhortation to refrain from such affairs. Obviously, the church was prone to hear what the pastor said, but not to heed his instruction.

Let us now after this be ashamed, and blush. A woman who had had five husbands, and who was of Samaria, was so eager concerning doctrines, that neither the time of day, nor her having come for another purpose, nor anything else, led her away from enquiring on such matters but we not only do not enquire concerning doctrines, but towards them all our dispositions are careless and indifferent. Therefore everything is neglected. For which of you when in his house takes some Christian book in hand and goes over its contents, and searches the Scriptures? None can say that he does so, but with most we shall find draughts and dice, but books nowhere, except among a few. And even these few have the same dispositions as the many; for they tie up their books, and keep them always put away in cases, and all their care is for the fineness of the parchments, and the beauty of the letters, not for reading them. For they have not bought them to obtain advantage and benefit from them, but take pains about such matters to show their wealth and pride. Such is the excess of vainglory. I do not hear any one glory that he knows the contents, but that he hath a book written in letters of gold. And what gain, tell me, is this? The Scriptures were not given us for this only, that we might have them in books, but that we might engrave them on our hearts. For this kind of possession, the keeping the commandments merely in letter, belongs to Jewish ambition; but to us the Law was not so given at all, but in the fleshy tables of our hearts. And this I say, not to prevent you from procuring Bibles, on the contrary, I exhort and earnestly pray that you do this, but I desire that from those books you convey the letters and sense into your understanding, that so it may be purified when it receives the meaning of the writing. For if the devil will not dare to approach a house where a Gospel is lying, much less will any evil spirit, or any sinful nature, ever touch or enter a soul which bears about with it such sentiments as it contains. Sanctify then your soul, sanctify your body, by having these ever in your heart, and on your tongue. For if foul speech defiles and invites devils, it is clear that spiritual reading sanctifies and draws down the grace of the Spirit. The Scriptures are divine charms, let us then apply to ourselves and to the passions of our souls the remedies to be derived from them. For if we understand what it is that is read, we shall hear it with much readiness. I am always saying this, and will not cease to say it. Is it not strange that those who sit by the market can tell the names, and families, and cities of charioteers, and dancers, and the kinds of power possessed by each, and can give exact account of the good or bad qualities of the very horses, but that those who come hither should know nothing of what is done here, but should be ignorant of the number even of the sacred Books? If you pursue those worldly things for pleasure, I will show you that here is greater pleasure. Which is sweeter, tell me, which more marvelous, to see a man wrestling with a man, or a man fighting with a devil, a body closing with an incorporeal power, and him who is of your race victorious? These wrestlings let us look on, these, which also it is seemly and profitable to imitate, and which imitating, we may be crowned; but not those in which emulation brings shame to him who imitates them. If you behold the one kind of contest, you behold it with devils; the other, with Angels and Archangels, and the Lord of Archangels. Say now, if you were allowed to sit with governors and kings, and to see and enjoy the spectacle, would you not deem it to be a very great honor? And here when you are a spectator in company with the King of Angels, when you see the devil grasped by the middle of the back, striving much to have the better, but powerless, do you not run and pursue after such a sight as this? "And how can this be?" said some one. If you keep the Bible in your hands; for in it you will see the lists, and the long races, and his grasps, and the skill of the righteous one. For by beholding these things you will learn also how to wrestle so yourself, and will escape clear of devils; the performances of the heathen are assemblies of devils, not theaters of men. Therefore I exhort you to abstain from these satanic assemblies; for if it is not lawful to enter into an idol's house, much less to Satan's festival. I shall not cease to say these things and weary you, until I see some change; for to say these things, as said Paul, "to me indeed is not grievous, but for you it is safe." Be not then offended at my exhortation. If any one ought to be offended, it is I who often speak and am not heard, not you who are always hearing and always disobeying. God grant that you be not always liable to this charge, but that freed from this shame you be deemed worthy to enjoy the spiritual spectacle, and the glory which is to come, through the grace and mercy of our Lord Jesus Christ, with whom to the Father and the Holy Spirit be glory for ever and ever. Amen.

NPNF 1.14, ed. Philip Schaff. Reprint, Peabody, MA: Hendrickson, 1994.

Augustine of Hippo (354–430)
Catechizing the Uninstructed

Writing in fifth-century North Africa, Augustine provided instruction for preaching in the church. An apparent problem the preacher faced was the audience's losing interest in the message. Augustine suggested that the preacher might try to insert a comment into his message to recapture the attention of the listeners. He warned that an attention-getting remark was not to distract from the overall direction of the sermon.

He also comments about some churches "across the sea" having seats for the attendants. This reference to practice on the other side of the Mediterranean from Augustine's North Africa demonstrates the diversity among congregations with regard to standing in worship services. Whereas in most places the congregation stood, there were places where seating was available. Augustine made allowance for those who grew tired from standing to be seated in his church.

19. It is likewise a frequent occurrence that one who at first listened to us with all readiness, becomes exhausted either by the effort of hearing or by standing, and now no longer commends what is said, but gapes and yawns, and even unwillingly exhibits a disposition to depart. When we observe that, it becomes our duty to refresh his mind by saying something seasoned with an honest cheerfulness and adapted to the matter that is being discussed, or something of a very wonderful and amazing order, or even, it may be, something of a painful and mournful nature. Whatever we thus

say may be all the better if it affects himself more immediately, so that the quick sense of self-concern may keep his attention on the alert. At the same time, however, it should not be of the kind to offend his spirit of reverence by any harshness attaching to it; but it should be of a nature fitted rather to conciliate him by the friendliness that it breathes. Or else, we should relieve him by accommodating him with a seat, although unquestionably matters will be better ordered if from the outset, whenever that can be done with propriety, he sits and listens. And indeed in certain of the churches beyond the sea, with a far more considerate regard to the fitness of things, not only do the prelates sit when they address the people, but they also themselves put down seats for the people, lest any person of enfeebled strength should become exhausted by standing, and thus have his mind diverted from the most wholesome purport of the discourse, or even be under the necessity of departing. . . . Nevertheless, supposing that we have once begun in that manner, we ought at least, whenever we observe signs of weariness on the part of the hearer, to offer him the liberty of being seated; nay more, we should urge him by all means to sit down, and we ought to drop some remark calculated at once to refresh him and to banish from his mind any anxiety which may have chanced to break in upon him and draw off his attention. For inasmuch as the reasons why he remains silent and declines to listen cannot be certainly known to us, now that he is seated we may speak to some extent against the incidence of thoughts about worldly affairs, delivering ourselves either in the cheerful spirit to which I have already adverted, or in a serious vein; so that, if these are the particular anxieties which have occupied his mind, they may be made to give way as if indicted by name: while, on the other hand, supposing them not to be the special causes of the loss of interest, and supposing him to be simply worn out with listening, his attention will be relieved of the pressure of weariness when we address to him some unexpected and extraordinary strain of remark on these subjects, in the mode of which I have spoken, as if they were the particular anxieties,—for indeed we are simply ignorant of the true causes. But let the remark thus made be short, especially considering that it is thrown in out of order, lest the very medicine even increase the malady of weariness which we desire to relieve; and, at the same time, we should go on rapidly with what remains, and promise and present the prospect of a conclusion nearer than was looked for.

NPNF 1.3, ed. Philip Schaff. Reprint, Peabody, MA: Hendrickson, 1994.

Augustine of Hippo (354–430)

On Christian Doctrine

Book Four of this work was meant as a manual for the Christian preacher. In it Augustine employed Cicero's instruction on rhetoric in his own teaching concerning proclamation of the Scriptures. Preaching involved three styles, each related to a particular purpose. The first style was reserved or somber, and was used to teach the congregation something it did not already know or had forgotten. The second style was that of beauty and was meant to make the message appealing to the people. The final style was persuasive, which exhorted the hearers to action. The mind, the heart, and the will were all to be targets of the preacher.

Augustine's picture of the effective preacher was somewhat different from John Chrysostom's. John, pastor in Constantinople, diminished the importance of style and rhetorical device, though he was nicknamed "the Golden-tongued" with respect to his own preaching. Augustine, on the other hand, as this selection demonstrates, believed that the pastor should use all the oratorical tools available to him. Eloquence was important because, he argued, the truth, which was sometimes bitter, would be more readily received if it were sweetened. Although the goal of the preacher was to teach the truth of the Scriptures in an eloquent and persuasive manner, wisdom was superior to oratorical skill.

Book Four

6. It is the duty, then, of the interpreter and teacher of Holy Scripture, the defender of the true faith and the opponent of error, both to teach what is right and to refute what is wrong, and in the performance of this task to conciliate the hostile, to rouse the careless, and to tell the ignorant both what is occurring at present and what is probable in the future. But once that his hearers are friendly, attentive, and ready to learn, whether he has found them so, or has himself made them so the remaining objects are to be carried out in whatever way the case requires. If the hearers need teaching, the matter treated of must be made fully known by means of narrative. On the other hand, to clear up points that are doubtful requires reasoning and the exhibition of proof. If, however, the hearers need to be roused rather than instructed, in order that they may be diligent to do what they already know, and

to bring their feelings into harmony with the truths they admit, greater vigor of speech is needed. Here entreaties and reproaches, exhortation and up-braiding, and all the other means of rousing the emotions, are necessary. . . .

8. Now it is especially necessary for the man who is bound to speak wisely, even though he cannot speak eloquently, to retain in memory the words of Scripture. For the more he discerns the poverty of his own speech, the more he ought to draw on the riches of Scripture, so that what he says in his own words he may prove by the words of Scripture; and he himself, though small and weak in his own words, may gain strength and power from the confirming testimony of great men. For his proof from Scripture gives pleasure even when his mode of speech does not. . . . And as we must often swallow wholesome bitters, so we must always avoid un-wholesome sweets. But what is better than wholesome sweetness or sweet wholesomeness? For the sweeter we try to make such things, the easier it is to make their wholesomeness serviceable. . . .

26. In the matter of teaching, of course, true eloquence consists not in making people like what they disliked, nor in making them do what they shrank from, but in making clear what was obscure. Yet if this be done with-out grace of style, the benefit does not extend beyond the few eager students who are anxious to know whatever is to be learned, however rude and un-polished the form in which it is put; and who, when they have succeeded in their object, find the plain truth to be pleasant food enough. And it is one of the distinctive features of good intellects not to love words, but the truth in words. For of what service is a golden key, if it cannot open what we want it to open? Or what objection is there to a wooden one if it can, seeing that to open what is shut is all we want? But as there is a certain analogy between learning and eating, the very food without which it is impossible to live must be flavored to meet the tastes of the majority. . . .

29. But for the sake of those who are so fastidious that they do not care for truth unless it is put in the form of a pleasing discourse, no small place has been assigned in eloquence to the art of pleasing. And yet even this is not enough for those stubborn-minded men who both understand and are pleased with the teacher's discourse, without deriving any profit from it. For what does it profit a man that he both confesses the truth and praises the elo-quence, if he does not yield his consent, when it is only for the sake of secur-ing his consent that the speaker in urging the truth gives careful attention to what he says? If the truths taught are such that to believe or to know them is enough, to give one's assent implies nothing more than to confess that they

are true. When, however, the truth taught is one that must be carried into practice, and that is taught for the very purpose of being practiced, it is useless to be persuaded of the truth of what is said, it is useless to be pleased with the manner in which it is said, if it be not so learnt as to be practiced. The eloquent preacher, then, when he is urging a practical truth, must not only teach so as to give instruction, and please so as to keep up the attention, but he must also sway the mind so as to subdue the will. For if a man be not moved by the force of truth, though it is demonstrated to his own confession, and clothed in beauty of style, nothing remains but to subdue him by the power of eloquence. . . .

32. And so our Christian orator, while he says what is just, and holy, and good (and he ought never to say anything else), does all he can to be heard with intelligence, with pleasure, and with obedience. He needs and so far as he succeeds, he will succeed more by piety in prayer than by gifts of oratory; and so he ought to pray for himself, and for those he is about to address, before he attempts to speak. And when the hour is come that he must speak, he ought, before he opens his mouth, to lift up his thirsty soul to God, to drink in what he is about to pour forth, and to be filled with what he is about to distribute. For, as in regard to every matter of faith and love there are many things that may be said, and many ways of saying them, who knows what it is expedient at a given moment for us to say, or to be heard saying, except God who knows the hearts of all? And who can make us say what we ought, and in the way we ought, except him in whose hand both we and our speeches are? Accordingly, he who is anxious both to know and to teach should learn all that is to be taught, and acquire such a faculty of speech as is suitable for a preacher. But when the hour for speech arrives, let him reflect upon that saying of our Lord's as better suited to the wants of a pious mind "Take no thought how or what you shall speak; for it shall be given you in that same hour what you shall speak. For it is not you that speaks, but the Spirit of your Father which speaks in you." The Holy Spirit, then, speaks thus in those who for Christ's sake are delivered to the persecutors; why not also in those who deliver Christ's message to those who are willing to learn? . . .

62. There are, indeed, some men who have a good delivery, but cannot compose anything to deliver. Now, if such men take what has been written with wisdom and eloquence by others, and commit it to memory, and deliver it to the people, they cannot be blamed, supposing them to do it without deception For in this way many become preachers of the truth

(which is certainly desirable), and yet not many teachers; for all deliver the discourse which one real teacher has composed, and there are no divisions among them.

NPNF 1.2, ed. Philip Schaff. Reprint, Peabody, MA: Hendrickson, 1994.

ADDITIONAL READINGS

Carroll, T. K. *Preaching the Word.* Wilmington, DE: Glazier, 1984.

Ferguson, E., ed. *The Bible in the Early Church,* Studies in Early Christianity, vol 3. New York: Garland, 1993.

Harmless, W. *Augustine and the Catechumenate.* Collegeville, MN: Liturgical, 1995.

Hunter, D. G., ed. *Preaching in the Patristic Age.* New York: Paulist, 1989.

Kerr, H. T. *Preaching in the Early Church.* New York: Revell, 1942.

Sider, R. D. *The Gospel and Its Proclamation.* Wilmington, DE: Glazier, 1983.

Toal, M. F. *The Sunday Sermons of the Great Fathers.* 4 vols. Chicago: Regnery, 1958–1963.

CHAPTER 4

Uniting the Community

The Eucharist in the Early Church

⅊

Toward the close of their services of worship, the Christians would share in the sacrament of the Eucharist. The term itself comes from the Greek for "thanksgiving," and referred to an offering of thanks to God for his redemption through Christ's death. The ordinance consisted of the eating of bread and drinking of wine in imitation of the meal Christ shared with his closest disciples/companions on the eve of his crucifixion. He instructed them to imitate his offering of bread and wine "in remembrance of him."

The rite was also known as the Lord's Supper and communion. The former title reminded participants that the "meal" was a representation of Christ's last supper with his disciples. In many instances, the Eucharist was a part of a larger meal known as an *agape,* or love feast. The latter title referred to the importance of the ceremony for the unity of the congregation. Often small groups would join together in homes to partake of the bread and wine. By sharing communion with one another, believers expressed their common faith and their membership within the Christian community. Only baptized members of the community were allowed to participate in the rite. Because the ceremony demonstrated the death of Christ, it demanded a particular reverence. Eventually, many Christians began to believe that the elements of the Lord's Supper were more than symbols of Christ's body and blood, but in fact were his body and blood.

Methods for administering the Eucharist vary in the written documents, and the statements and prayers to be said by the minister differ in particular contexts. Sometimes the ceremony was part of a meal attended by the church. Often small groups in homes took the Lord's Supper. The days on which the rite should be administered, those who were allowed to partake in it, what should be said, and what type of bread and wine should be used were each concerns of the early church.

The Didache (Early Second Century)

One finds in this work three important ideas about the Eucharist. First, it was a reminder of the redemptive work of God in Christ. The communicant offered thanks to God for this salvation. Second, the ceremony was intended to create unity within the community, linking the practice of the Lord's Supper with the shared faith of the Christians. Finally, because the rite united believers with one another, only baptized members of the church were to participate.

Chapter Nine

Now concerning the Eucharist, offer thanks in this way. First, concerning the cup say, "We thank you, our Father, for the holy vine of David your servant, which you made known to us through Jesus your servant. To you be the glory for ever." And concerning the broken bread say, "We thank you, our Father, for the life and knowledge which you made known to us through Jesus your servant. To you be the glory for ever. Even as this broken bread was scattered over the hills, and was gathered together and became one, so let your church be gathered together from the ends of the earth into your kingdom; for yours is the glory and the power through Jesus Christ for ever." But let no one eat or drink of your Eucharist, but they who have been baptized into the name of the Lord. For concerning this also the Lord said, "Give not that which is holy to the dogs."

ANF 7, ed. A. Cleveland Coxe. Reprint, Peabody, MA: Hendrickson, 1994.

Ignatius of Antioch (35–107)
To the Philadelphians

In this passage from his letter to the church in Philadelphia in Asia Minor, penned en route to martyrdom in Rome, Ignatius' primary concern is the unity of the church. This union of believers within the community is illustrated by the one cup and one loaf of the Lord's Supper. The purpose of the meal is to produce the unity of the church, called the one Body of Christ.

Chapter Two

As children of light and truth, flee from division and heresy; but where the shepherd is, there the sheep follow. For there are many wolves that appear worthy of honor, who, by means of pernicious pleasure carry away those who are running towards God; but in your unity they will have no place.

Chapter Three

Keep yourselves from those evil plants that Jesus Christ does not tend, as they are not the planting of the Father. It is not that I have found any schism among you, but rather exceeding purity. For as many as are of God and of Jesus Christ, are also with the bishop. And as many as shall, in the exercise of repentance return to unity with the church, these also shall belong to God, in order that they may live according to Jesus Christ. Do not err, brothers and sisters. If anyone follows him that makes a schism in the church he will not inherit the Kingdom of God. If anyone walks according to heresy, he does not agree with the suffering of Christ.

Chapter Four

I have confidence of you in the Lord that you will be of no other mind. Therefore I write boldly to your love, which is worthy of God, and exhort you to have but one faith, and one preaching, and one Eucharist. For there is one flesh of the Lord Jesus Christ; and his blood which was shed for us is one. One loaf also is broken to all the communicants, and one cup is distributed among them all. There is but one altar for the whole Church, and one bishop, with the presbytery and deacons, my fellow-servants.

ANF 1, ed. A. Cleveland Coxe. Reprint, Peabody, MA: Hendrickson, 1994.

Ignatius of Antioch (35–107)

To the Smyrnaeans

Ignatius' purpose for writing the letter to the Christians in the Asia Minor city of Smyrna was to encourage them to "follow the bishop" with regard to the Eucharist. In this selection, he teaches them that the Lord's Supper was to be properly observed only under the authority of the bishop. This was not to imply that the proper Eucharist was one administered *only* by the bishop, because he adds that it could be someone whom he entrusted to do so. Rather, he was writing to confront schism and rebellion against the bishop. His point was not in the perceived worth of the bishop to administer the sacrament, but in the need for all things related to the life of the church, in this instance the Eucharist, to be under the authority of the church's overseer.

Chapter Eight

See that you all follow the bishop, even as Christ Jesus does the Father, and the presbytery as you would the apostles. You should also reverence the deacons, as those that carry out through their office the appointment of God. Let no man do anything connected with the Church without the bishop. Let that be deemed a proper Eucharist, which is administered either by the bishop, or by one to whom he has entrusted it. Wherever the bishop shall appear, there let the multitude of the people also be; even as where Christ is, there does all the heavenly host stand by, waiting upon him as the Chief Captain of the Lord's might, and the Governor of every intelligent nature. It is not lawful without the bishop either to baptize, or to offer, or to present sacrifice, or to celebrate a love-feast. But that which seems good to him, is also well-pleasing to God, that everything you do may be secure and valid.

ANF 1, ed. A. Cleveland Cox. Reprint, Peabody, MA: Hendrickson, 1994.

Justin Martyr (110–165)

First Apology

According to Justin Martyr, only those who had previously been baptized for the remission of their sins were allowed to participate in the Eucharist because only they were allowed to become members of the Christian church, as was seen in chapter 1. He emphasized that believers were to see this ceremony as a genuinely spiritual occasion, so that while they were partaking of the bread and wine, they were to be thinking of the body and blood Christ offered for their salvation.

Chapter Sixty-Five

After the one who has become convinced of our teaching and vowed to live according to it has been washed, we bring him to the place where the brothers and sisters are assembled, so that we may offer hearty prayers together for ourselves and the newly baptized, and for all others in every place. This is so we may be counted worthy, now that we have learned the truth, and that by our works we may be found to be good citizens and keepers of the commandments, in order to be saved with an eternal salvation. Once we have ended the prayers, we salute one another with a kiss. Then the bread and a cup of wine mixed with water is brought out. After giving praise and glory to the Father of the universe, through the name of the Son and the Holy Spirit, for a long time thanks are offered for our being counted worthy to receive these things at his hands. When these prayers and thanksgivings are finished, all those present express their assent by saying Amen, which in Hebrew means "so be it." When the one presiding has given thanks, and all the people have expressed their assent, the deacons give to each of those present some of the bread and the wine mixed with water over which the thanksgiving was pronounced. A portion of each element is taken to those who are absent.

Chapter Sixty-Six

And this food is called among us the Eucharist, of which no one is allowed to partake but the man who believes that the things which we teach are true, and who has been washed with the washing that is for the remission of sins, and unto regeneration, and who is so living as Christ has instructed. For not as common bread and common drink do we receive these; but in like manner as Jesus Christ our Savior, having been made flesh by the Word of God, had both flesh and blood for our salvation, so likewise have we been taught that the food which is blessed by the prayer of his word, and from which our blood and flesh by transmutation are nourished, is the flesh and blood of that

Jesus who was made flesh. For the apostles, in the memoirs composed by them, which are called Gospels, have thus delivered unto us what was instructed to them: that Jesus took bread, and when he had given thanks, said, "Do this in remembrance of me, this is my body." In the same manner, having taken the cup and given thanks, he said, "This is my blood," and gave it to them alone. The wicked devils have imitated this in the mysteries of Mithras, commanding the same thing to be done. For, that bread and a cup of water are placed with certain incantations in the mystic rites of one who is being initiated, you either know or can learn.

ANF 1, ed. A. Cleveland Coxe. Reprint, Peabody, MA: Hendrickson, 1994.

Minucius Felix (Second or Third Century)
The Octavius

Felix is a late second- or early-third-century apologist writing in Rome, who sought to explain Christian belief and practice to a pagan audience. His primary objective was to convince his friend Caecilius of the validity of Christianity.

This selection reveals something of the conception held by some outside of the church regarding the Eucharist. Felix defends Christianity against the notion that the Christian initiation rite called for the slaughter of an infant, and the drinking of his blood. He contends that Christians had great concern for their children, unlike many pagans, whose practice of exposure or strangling had brought death to many unwanted children. Felix's response shows the importance of interpreting the statements about the body and blood of Christ figuratively. A literal reading of the terms left Christians open to the charge of cannibalism.

Chapter Nine

The story about the initiation of young converts is as much to be detested as it is well known. An infant is covered over with meal in order to deceive the unwary. The infant is placed before the one who is to be stained with their rites. He is then slain by the young pupil, who has been urged on as if he is striking harmless blows on the surface of the meal; however there are dark and secret wounds. What horror as they lick up its blood, eagerly dividing its limbs! By this victim they are pledged together; with this consciousness of wickedness they are covenanted to mutual silence. Such sacred rites as these are more foul than any sacrileges.

Chapter Thirty

And now I should wish to respond to the one who says or believes that we are initiated by the slaughter and blood of an infant. Do you think that it can be possible for such a tender, little body to receive those fatal wounds, and for anyone to shed, pour forth, and drain that new blood of a youngling? Do you believe that such a man exists? No one can believe this, except one who can dare to do it. And I see that you at one time expose your begotten children to wild beasts and to birds; at another, that you crush them when strangled with a miserable kind of death. There are some women who, by drinking medical preparations, extinguish the source of the future person in their very bowels, and thus commit a parricide before they bring forth. And these things assuredly come down from the teaching of your gods. For Saturn did not expose his children, but devoured them. With reason were infants sacrificed to him by parents in some parts of Africa, caresses and kisses repressing their crying, that a weeping victim might not be sacrificed. Moreover, among the Tauri of Pontus, and to the Egyptian Busiris, it was a sacred rite to immolate their guests, and for the Galli to slaughter to Mercury human, or rather inhuman, sacrifices. The Romans sacrificed by burying alive a Greek man and a Greek woman, a Gallic man and a Gallic woman; and to this day, Jupiter Latiaris is worshipped by them with murder; and, what is worthy of the son of Saturn, he is gorged with the blood of an evil and criminal man. I believe that he himself taught Catiline to conspire under a compact of blood, and Bellona to steep her sacred rites with a draught of human gore, and taught men to heal epilepsy with the blood of a man, that is, with a worse disease. They also are not unlike to him who devour the wild beasts from the arena, besmeared and stained with blood, or fattened with the limbs or the entrails of men. To us it is not lawful either to see or to hear of homicide; and so much do we shrink from human blood, that we do not use the blood even of eatable animals in our food.

ANF 4, ed. A. Cleveland Coxe. Reprint, Peabody, MA: Hendrickson, 1994.

Irenaeus of Lyons (115–202)

Against Heresies

This bishop of Lyons focused most of his writing on refuting the teachings of Gnosticism. Here he confronts the Gnostic notion that only the spiritual element of humanity is to be saved, and not the physical. The heresy also denied the Incarnation, claiming that Christ only *appeared* to be a human being.[1] If Jesus was not God who lived a genuinely human life, then the message contained in the Eucharist is nullified. If the body and blood of Christ were not genuine, there would be no benefit in "remembering" them through the elements of the Lord's Supper. In partaking of the bread and the wine—referred to as the mingled cup, i.e., mixture of water and wine—one's flesh was nourished by the flesh of Christ, and one received eternal life.

Book Five, Chapter Two

2. But vain in every respect are they who despise the entire dispensation of God, and disallow the salvation of the flesh, and treat with contempt its regeneration, maintaining that it is not capable of incorruption. But if this indeed does not attain salvation, then neither did the Lord redeem us with his blood, nor is the cup of the Eucharist the communion of his blood, nor the bread which we break the communion of his body. For blood can only come from veins and flesh, and whatsoever else makes up the substance of human beings, such as the Word of God was actually made. By his own blood he redeemed us, as also his apostle declares, "In whom we have redemption through his blood, even the remission of sins." And as we are his members, we are also nourished by means of the creation—and he himself grants the creation to us, for he causes his sun to rise, and sends rain when he wills. He has acknowledged the cup—which is a part of the creation—as his own blood, from which he bedews our blood; and the bread—also a part of the creation—he has established as his own body, from which he gives increase to our bodies.

3. When, therefore, the mingled cup and the manufactured bread receives the Word of God, and the Eucharist of the blood and the body of Christ is made, from which things the substance of our flesh is increased and supported, how can they affirm that the flesh, which is nourished from the body

and blood of the Lord, and is a member of him, is incapable of receiving the gift of God, which is eternal life? The blessed Paul declares this in his Letter to the Ephesians: "We are members of his body, of his flesh, and of his bones." He does not speak these words of some spiritual and invisible man, for a spirit has not bones nor flesh; but he refers to that dispensation by which the Lord became an actual human being, consisting of flesh, and nerves, and bones. He speaks of that flesh which is nourished by the cup which is his blood, and receives increase from the bread which is his body.

ANF 1, ed. A. Cleveland Coxe. Reprint, Peabody, MA: Hendrickson, 1994.

Cyprian of Carthage (200–258)

Letter 62

In this letter, Cyprian, pastor of the Christian community at Carthage, addressed the question of whether water was appropriate to use in observing the Eucharist. His conclusion was that water was not a valid substitute for the traditional drink: water mixed with wine. His reasoning was twofold. First, both Jesus' institution of the Lord's Supper and Paul's teaching in his letter to the Corinthians instructed that wine was to be used. Second, the purpose of drinking from the cup was to remind the participant of the blood of Christ, whose sacrifice was for their redemption. When the communicant saw and tasted the wine, he or she was reminded of the shedding of Jesus' blood.

Another theme Cyprian addressed was that of martyrdom. He wrote this letter during Decius' persecution of Christians, the first empirewide, systematic persecution. He implies that it would be difficult for one to sacrifice his or her own blood if unwilling to drink the blood of Christ. It is probable that Cyprian was using a rhetorical device to inspire his readers to conform to the traditional practice, rather than making a theological statement concerning the salvific effects of the Eucharist. If someone were repulsed at drinking wine merely resembling blood, how much more difficult it would have been for that person to actually shed his or her own blood.

2. Know then that I have been admonished that in offering the cup the tradition of the Lord must be observed, and that nothing must be done by us but what the Lord first did on our behalf, as that the cup which is offered in

remembrance of Him should be offered mingled with wine. For when Christ says, "I am the true vine," the blood of Christ is assuredly not water, but wine. Neither can his blood by which we are redeemed and given life appear to be in the cup, when in the cup there is no wine whereby the blood of Christ is shown forth, which is declared by the sacrament and testimony of all the Scriptures. . . .

10. Moreover, the blessed Apostle Paul, chosen and sent by the Lord, and appointed a preacher of the Gospel truth, lays down these very things in his epistle, saying, "The Lord Jesus, the same night in which he was be-trayed, took bread; and when he had given thanks, he broke it, and said, 'This is my body, which shall be given for you: do this in remembrance of me.' After the same manner also he took the cup, when he had dined, say-ing, 'This cup is the new testament in my blood: this do, as often as you drink it, in remembrance of me.' For as often as you eat this bread and drink this cup, you shall show forth the Lord's death until he comes." If it is both instructed by the Lord, and the same thing is confirmed and deliv-ered by his apostle, that as often as we drink, we do in remembrance of the Lord the same thing which the Lord also did, we find that what was com-manded is not observed by us, unless we also do what the Lord did; and that mixing the Lord's cup in like manner we do not depart from the di-vine teaching; but that we must not at all depart from the evangelical pre-cepts, and that disciples ought also to observe and to do the same things which the Master both taught and did. The blessed apostle in another place more earnestly and strongly teaches, saying, "I marvel that you are so soon removed from him that called you into grace, unto another gospel, which is not another. There are some that trouble you, and would pervert the Gospel of Christ. But though we, or an angel from heaven, preach any-thing other than that which we have preached to you, let him be anath-ema. As we said before, so say I now again, If any man preach any other gospel unto you than that you have received, let him be anathema." . . .

15. But the discipline of all religion and truth is overturned unless what is spiritually prescribed be faithfully observed; unless indeed any one should fear in the morning sacrifices, lest by the taste of wine he should be redolent of the blood of Christ. Therefore thus the brotherhood is beginning even to be kept back from the passion of Christ in persecutions, by learning in the offerings to be disturbed concerning his blood and his blood-shedding. Moreover, however, the Lord says in the Gospel, "Whosoever shall be

ashamed of me, of him shall the Son of man be ashamed." And the apostle also speaks, saying, "If I pleased men, I should not be the servant of Christ." But how can we shed our blood for Christ, if we blush at drinking the blood of Christ?

16. Does any one perchance flatter himself with this notion, that although in the morning, water alone is seen to be offered, yet when we come to supper we offer the mingled cup? But when we dine, we cannot call the people together to our banquet, so as to celebrate the truth of the sacrament in the presence of all the brotherhood. But still it was not in the morning, but after dinner, that the Lord offered the mingled cup. Ought we then to celebrate the Lord's cup after supper, that so by continual repetition of the Lord's Supper we may offer the mingled cup? It behooved Christ to offer about the evening of the day, that the very hour of sacrifice might show the setting and the evening of the world; as it is written in Exodus, "And all the people of the synagogue of the children of Israel shall kill it in the evening." And again in the Psalms, "Let the lifting up of my hands be an evening sacrifice." But we celebrate the resurrection of the Lord in the morning.

ANF 5, ed. A. Cleveland Coxe. Reprint, Peabody, MA: Hendrickson, 1994.

Basil of Caesarea (330–379)

Letter 93

Basil wrote this letter in 372 in order to address the question of when to participate in communion. The author encouraged his readers to participate in the Eucharist often, even to the point of doing so daily. He did so himself at least four times a week, and perhaps more if a special occasion warranted it. It was not necessary that a bishop or other officer of the church administer the sacrament. He cited times of persecution and desert monks as examples of when this might occur. He did not, it seems, cite these as exceptions to a rigorous requirement, but as proof that no strict requirement existed. Moreover, in Egypt many believers kept portions of the elements at home for private practice of the rite. Even in the assembly communicants used their own hands to take the elements. Basil's emphasis was on the faith of the recipient rather than on the worth or value of the one who administered the bread and the cup.

It is good and beneficial to participate in communion every day, and to partake of the holy body and blood of Christ. For he distinctly says, "He that eats my flesh and drinks my blood has eternal life." And who doubts that to share frequently in life, is the same thing as to have manifold life. I, indeed, communicate four times a week: on the Lord's Day, on Wednesday, on Friday, and on the Sabbath; and on other days if there is a commemoration of any saint. It is needless to point out that for anyone in times of persecution to be compelled to take the communion in his own hand without the presence of a priest or minister is not a serious offense, as long custom sanctions this practice from the facts themselves. All the solitaries in the desert, where there is no priest, take the communion themselves, keeping communion at home. At Alexandria and in Egypt, each one of the laity, for the most part, keeps the communion, at his own house, and participates in it when he wills. For when once the priest has completed the offering, and given it, the recipient, participating in it each time as entire, is bound to believe that he properly takes and receives it from the giver. And even in the church, when the priest gives the portion, the recipient takes it with complete power over it, and so lifts it to his lips with his own hand. It has the same validity whether one portion or several portions are received from the priest at the same time.

NPNF 2.8, ed. W. Sanday. Reprint, Peabody, MA: Hendrickson, 1994.

Cyril of Jerusalem (315–386)
Catechetical Lecture 22

Cyril saw in Christ's statement to eat his flesh and drink his blood for eternal life an obvious reference to the ordinance of the Eucharist. The statement was to be taken "spiritually," however, and not literally. In his catechetical lectures he interpreted this to mean that although one ate bread and drank wine, by faith one received Christ and became a partaker in the divine nature.

3. Wherefore with full assurance let us partake as of the body and blood of Christ: for in the figure of bread is given to you his body, and in the figure of wine his blood; that you by partaking of the body and blood of Christ, may be made of the same body and the same blood with him. For in this way we come to bear Christ in us, because his body and blood are distributed

through our members. Therefore, it is in that way, according to the blessed Peter, we became partakers of the divine nature.

4. Christ on a certain occasion discoursing with the Jews said, 'Except you eat my flesh and drink my blood, you have no life in you.' Because they did not hear his saying in a spiritual sense were offended, and went back, supposing that he was inviting them to eat flesh. . . .

6. Consider therefore the bread and the wine not as bare elements; for they are, according to the Lord's declaration, the body and blood of Christ. Even though sense suggests this to you, yet let faith establish you. Judge not the matter from the taste, but from faith be fully assured without misgiving, that the body and blood of Christ have been given to you.

NPNF 2.7, ed. W. Sanday. Reprint, Peabody, MA: Hendrickson, 1994.

Jerome (347–420)

Letter 71

Jerome is perhaps best known for his Latin translation of the Bible, called the *Vulgate*. He also translated a number of Origen's writings and Pachomius' *Rule* (a pattern for monastic living) from Greek into Latin. In addition, he produced a number of commentaries on the Bible, polemical writings against various parties, a biographical collection called *On the Lives of Illustrious Men,* and a significant collection of correspondence. Jerome also founded a monastery in Bethlehem in 386 after being forced out of Rome by the new bishop, presumably because of Jerome's strict ascetical practice and teaching.

The author shows how the tradition of the time was to fast on the Sabbath and participate in communion daily. He instructed that while it was appropriate to follow this custom, particular churches should not have felt compelled to follow only one pattern. Jerome indicated that his readers could receive the Eucharist at any time, not simply on specific days or during particular seasons. There seems to have been no defined and rigorous practice for when to celebrate the Lord's Supper.

6. You ask me whether you ought to fast on the Sabbath and to receive the Eucharist daily according to the custom—as currently reported—of the churches of Rome and Spain. Both these points have been treated by the

eloquent Hippolytus, and several writers have collected passages from differ-ent authors bearing upon them. The best advice that I can give you is this. Church-traditions—especially when they do not run counter to the faith—are to be observed in the form in which previous generations have handed them down; and the use of one church is not to be annulled because it is con-trary to that of another. As regards fasting, I wish that we could practice it without intermission as—according to the Acts of the Apostles—Paul did and the believers with him even in the season of Pentecost and on the Lord's Day. They are not to be accused of Manicheeism, for carnal food ought not to be preferred before spiritual. As regards the holy Eucharist you may receive it at all times without qualm of conscience or disapproval from me. You may listen to the psalmist's words: —"O taste and see that the Lord is good;" you may sing as he does: —"my heart pours forth a good word." But do not mis-take my meaning. You are not to fast on feast-days, neither are you to abstain on the week days in Pentecost. In such matters each province may follow its own inclinations, and the traditions which have been handed down should be regarded as apostolic laws.

NPNF 2.6, ed. W. Sanday. Reprint, Peabody, MA: Hendrickson, 1994.

John Chrysostom of Constantinople (347–407)
Homily 3 on Ephesians

John's sermons on numerous books of the Bible are a tribute to his ministry. This sermon on Ephesians is representative of the many homilies he preached while in Constantinople. In the selection he instructed that only those who had been baptized were to participate in the Eucharist. In fact, those not baptized were not even to be present. The central theme of the se-lection is that communicants were to be undefiled and pure in their living. In describing the Eucharist, John speaks of songs and prayers which pre-pared the people for receiving the ordinance, just as servants would have cleaned the tables in one's home in preparation for a banquet. Here is the twofold emphasis on the importance of the Lord's Supper both for the in-dividual and for the community.

I observe many partaking of Christ's body lightly only out of rote tradition and practice rather than with due consideration and understanding. Whenever the holy season of Lent or the Feast of the Lord's Epiphany come, whatever someone might be, he partakes of the mysteries. Yet it is neither the Epiphany nor Lent that makes it appropriate to approach the Eucharist, but the sincerity and purity of the soul. . . . How will you present yourself before the judgment seat of Christ when you have presumed upon his body with polluted hands and lips? You would not presume to kiss a king with an unclean mouth, yet you kiss the King of heaven with an unclean soul? It is an outrage. . . .

As it is not fitting that someone who has not been initiated through baptism be present in the Eucharist, so neither is it fitting that one who has been initiated but is defiled should be present. Tell me, suppose someone were invited to a feast, and were to wash his hands, and sit down, and be ready at the table, and after all refuse to partake. Is he not insulting the one who invited him? Were it not better for such an one never to have come at all? Now it is just in the same way that you have come here. You have sung the hymn with the rest: you have declared yourself to be of the number of them who are worthy, by not departing with them that are not worthy. Why stay, and yet not partake of the table? I am unworthy, you will say. Then are you also unworthy of that communion you have had in prayers. For it is not by means of the offerings only, but also by means of those canticles that the Spirit descends around. For we not see our own servants, first scouring the table with a sponge, and cleaning the house, and then setting out the entertainment? This is what is done by the prayers, and by the cry of the herald. We scour the Church, as it were, with a sponge, that all things may be set out in a pure church, that there may be "neither spot nor wrinkle." Unworthy indeed, both our eyes of these sights, and unworthy are our ears! . . . You are no more allowed here than the catechumen is. For it is not at all the same thing never to have reached the mysteries, and when you have reached them, to stumble at them and despise them, and to me yourself unworthy of this thing. One might enter upon more points, and those more awful still; not however to burden your understanding, these will suffice. They who are not brought to their right senses with these, certainly will not be with more.

NPNF 1.13, ed. Philip Schaff. Reprint, Peabody, MA: Hendrickson, 1994.

ADDITIONAL READINGS

Crockett, W. R. *Eucharist: Symbol of Transformation.* New York: Pueblo, 1989.

Ferguson, E., ed. *Worship in Early Christianity,* Studies in Early Christianity, vol. 15. New York: Garland, 1993.

Keating, J. *The Agape and the Eucharist in the Early Church: Studies in the History of the Christian Love-Feasts.* London: Methuen, 1901.

Kilmartin, J. *The Eucharist in the Primitive Church.* Englewood Cliffs, NJ: Prentice-Hall, 1965.

Mazza, E. *The Celebration of the Eucharist: The Origin of the Rite and the Development of Its Interpretation,* trans. M. J. O'Connell. Collegeville, MN: Liturgical, 1999.

McGowan, A. *Ascetic Eucharists: Food and Drink in Early Christian Ritual Meals.* Oxford Early Christian Studies. New York: Oxford University Press, 1999.

Sheerin, D. J. *The Eucharist.* Wilmington, DE: Glazier, 1986.

Wainwright, G. *Eucharist and Eschatology.* New York: Oxford University Press, 1981.

Weil, L. *Sacraments and Liturgy: The Outward Signs.* Oxford: Blackwell, 1983.

CHAPTER 5

Expanding the Community

Evangelism in the Early Church

⁂

The Christian community began as a small number of Jews dedicating themselves to follow a rabbi named Jesus of Nazareth. They came to believe that this teacher was the Messiah promised in the Hebrew Bible (what Christians call the Old Testament). In a short period of time, despite some localized persecution, this community grew to comprise people from most regions of the Roman Empire. The extraordinary growth of the church from humble beginnings to the dominant religion in the empire after Constantine's conversion was the result of its desire to include others by preaching its message, which the Christians called the Gospel, or Good News, of Jesus Christ.

Christians attempted to convert their neighbors and others through evangelism, or the personal proclamation of the teachings of Christ. They did this not simply by sharing the message of Jesus but also by living a life that demonstrated their own conversion. The ability of Christianity to change an individual from being wicked to being moral was one of the most important elements of the church's message.

Though the community did thrive, it faced obstacles, including society's (mis)understanding of the Christian message. We have already seen Minucius Felix's attempts to deny the accusation that Christians sacrificed infants in their celebration of the Eucharist. In this chapter we find that two representative apologists, Tertullian of Carthage and Origen of Alexandria, defended the community against charges amounting to treason. They wrote of the changes made in the lives of believers as they responded to the church's message. In each instance, they attempted to convince their readers that the Christian faith was not speculative philosophy or a danger to society, but was the one means to fellowship with God.

During times of persecution, whether sanctioned by the government or merely proceeding from anti-Christian bigotry in society, the church actually grew in number and expanded in its reach. Tertullian explained that the increase was due to the influence martyrs' faith had on witnesses to their deaths. Rather than frightening those who saw the suffering and convincing them either to abandon or to reject the faith, oppression caused many to take up the cause. This led Tertullian to conclude that the blood of the martyrs was the seed of the church, meaning that martyrdom typically, and ironically, produced an increase in the community.

In both Origen and John Chrysostom of Constantinople, one discovers that members of the community were expected to long for and attempt to produce the conversion of all classes and races to Christianity. Expansion of the church was to be desired and pursued. Christians sought to convince others of the validity of their message through proclamation of the teachings of Christ and by practicing exemplary moral living, which potentially meant suffering martyrdom for their faith. Both the perceived responsibility and the hope of the community was its expansion through the conversion of family, friends, and neighbors.

Justin *Martyr* (110–165)
Dialogue with Trypho

In this fictitious "dialogue," written in the second century, the apologist Justin Martyr contrasted Judaism and Christianity, attempting to demonstrate the superiority of the latter over the former. He concluded that the task of proclaiming the message of God (i.e., the "prophetical gifts") rested no longer with the Jews but with the Christians. This community was responsible for presenting salvation to those outside the church, or faced chastisement from God for not doing so. Therefore, it sought diligently to convince others of the validity of its message. Justin wrote this dialogue to explain that the ministry of the church, a ministry that had once belonged to the Jews, was to warn others of their sin. Early Christians expected believers to attempt to expand the community through preaching a message of salvation from sin and reconciliation with God.

Chapter Eighty-Two

For the prophetical gifts remain with us, even to the present time. Therefore you should understand that the gifts formerly among your nation have been transferred to us. And just as there were false prophets contemporary with your holy prophets, so are there now many false teachers among us, of whom our Lord forewarned us to beware. In no way are we deficient, since we know that he foreknew all that would happen to us after his resurrection from the dead and ascension to heaven. For he said we would be put to death, and hated for his name's sake; and that many false prophets and false christs would appear in his name, and deceive many: and so has it come about. For many have taught godless, blasphemous, and unholy doctrines, forging them in his name; have taught, too, and even yet are teaching, those things which proceed from the unclean spirit of the devil, and which were put into their hearts. Therefore we are most anxious that you be persuaded not to be misled by such persons, since we know that every one who can speak the truth, and yet speaks it not, shall be judged by God, as God testified by Ezekiel, when he said, "I have made you a watchman to the house of Judah. If the sinner sin, and you warn him not, he himself shall die in his sin; but his blood will I require at your hand. But if you warn him, you shall be innocent." And on this account we are, through fear, very earnest in desiring to converse with men according to the Scriptures, but not from love of money, or of glory, or of pleasure. For no man can convict us of any of these vices.

ANF 1, ed. A. Cleveland Coxe. Reprint, Peabody, MA: Hendrickson, 1994.

Irenaeus of Lyons (115–202)

Against Heresies

Here we find this second-century opponent of the Gnostics articulating the one message of the Christian faith, which had by this time been accepted throughout the Roman Empire. Though there were different peoples who had accepted the teaching of Christianity, these particular groups did not constitute distinct communities that were severed from one another. Rather, there was for Irenaeus only one universal community, called the church. Most instructive in this selection is the extent to which it may be seen that Christianity had spread into different places, including regions such as Germany and Libya. From this expansion one can see that the early believers were at least somewhat effective in bringing others into the church. They did this by preaching the same message regardless of their location.

Book One, Chapter Ten

1. The Church, though dispersed through our the whole world, even to the ends of the earth, has received from the apostles and their disciples this faith: She believes in one God, the Father Almighty, Maker of heaven, and earth, and the sea, and all things that are in them; and in one Christ Jesus, the Son of God, who became incarnate for our salvation; and in the Holy Spirit, who proclaimed through the prophets the dispensations of God, and the advents, and the birth from a virgin, and the passion, and the resurrection from the dead, and the ascension into heaven in the flesh of the beloved Christ Jesus, our Lord, and his future manifestation from heaven in the glory of the Father "to gather all things in one," and to raise up anew all flesh of the whole human race, in order that to Christ Jesus, our Lord, and God, and Savior, and King, according to the will of the invisible Father, "every knee should bow, of things in heaven, and things in earth, and things under the earth, and that every tongue should confess" to him, and that he should execute just judgment towards all; that he may send "spiritual wickednesses," and the angels who transgressed and became apostates, together with the ungodly, and unrighteous, and wicked, and profane among men, into everlasting fire; but may, in the exercise of his grace, confer immortality on the righteous, and holy, and those who have kept his commandments, and have persevered in his love, some from the beginning of their Christian course, and others from the date of their repentance, and may surround them with everlasting glory.

2. As I have already observed, the Church, having received this preaching and this faith, although scattered throughout the whole world, yet, as if occupying but one house, carefully preserves it. She also believes these points of doctrine just as if she had but one soul, and one and the same heart, and she proclaims them, and teaches them, and hands them down, with perfect harmony, as if she possessed only one mouth. For, although the languages of the world are dissimilar, yet the import of the tradition is one and the same. For the Churches which have been planted in Germany do not believe or hand

down anything different, nor do those in Spain, nor those in Gaul, nor those in the East, nor those in Egypt, nor those in Libya, nor those which have been established in the central regions of the world. But as the sun, that creature of God, is one and the same throughout the whole world, so also the preaching of the truth shines everywhere, and enlightens all men that are willing to come to a knowledge of the truth. Nor will any one of the rulers in the Churches, however highly gifted he may be in point of eloquence, teach doctrines different from these—for no one is greater than the Master—nor, on the other hand, will he who is deficient in power of expression inflict injury on the tradition. For the faith being ever one and the same, neither does one who is able at great length to discourse regarding it, make any addition to it, nor does one, who can say but little diminish it.

ANF 1, ed. A. Cleveland Coxe. Reprint, Peabody, MA: Hendrickson, 1994.

Tertullian of Carthage (160–212)
Apology

Writing to explain Christianity to its opponents, Tertullian here challenges the persecution of Christians by the state, which appeared to him to be counterproductive for the enemies of the church. First, people who had broken no law, but had been exemplary citizens and productive members of society, were jailed and/or killed. Second, the number of Christians was so great by this point that if they all were killed the empire would have been subject to an easy defeat by its enemies. Tertullian provides details about the spread of the faith among every part of society: the only place where Christians were not to be found was the pagan temple. As Irenaeus had previously indicated, no social or economic class had been unreached. Finally, the persecution that sought to destroy the church was in fact a means to its continued growth. Members of the community were willing to face martyrdom precisely because a martyr's death produced greater commitment among others and persuaded many to become Christians. Here we find Tertullian's famous dictum: "The more we are mown down by you the more in number we grow; the blood of the Christians is seed." He believed persecution had aided rather than slowed the expansion of the community.

Chapter Thirty-Seven

If we are enjoined, then, to love our enemies, as I have remarked above, whom have we to hate? If injured, we are forbidden to retaliate, lest we become as bad ourselves: who can suffer injury at our hands? In regard to this, recall your own experiences. How often you inflict gross cruelties on Christians, partly because it is your own inclination, and partly in obedience to the laws! How often, too, the hostile mob, paying no regard to you, takes the law into its own hand, and assails us with stones and flames, they do not even spare the Christian dead, but tear them, now sadly changed, no longer entire, from the rest of the tomb, from the asylum we might say of death, cutting them in pieces, rending them asunder. Yet, banded together as we are, ever so ready to sacrifice our lives, what single case of revenge for injury are you able to point to, though, if it were held right among us to repay evil by evil, a single night with a torch or two could achieve an ample vengeance? But away with the idea of a sect divine avenging itself by human fires, or shrinking from the sufferings in which it is tried. If we desired, indeed, to act the part of open enemies, not merely of secret avengers, would there be any lacking in strength, whether of numbers or resources? . . . We are but of yesterday, and we have filled every place among you—cities, islands, fortresses, towns, market-places, the very camp, tribes, companies, palace, senate, forum; we have left nothing to you but the temples of your gods. For what wars should we not be fit, not eager, even with unequal forces, we who so willingly yield ourselves to the sword, if in our religion it were not counted better to be slain than to slay? Without arms even, and raising no insurrectionary banner, but simply in enmity to you, we could carry on the contest with you by an ill-willed severance alone. For if such multitudes of men were to break away from you, and betake themselves to some remote corner of the world, why, the very loss of so many citizens, whatever sort they were, would cover the empire with shame; nay, in the very forsaking, vengeance would be inflicted. Why, you would be horror-struck at the solitude in which you would find yourselves, at such an all-prevailing silence, and that stupor as of a dead world. You would have to seek subjects to govern. You would have more enemies than citizens remaining. For now it is the immense number of Christians which makes your enemies so few, almost all the inhabitants of your various cities being followers of Christ. Yet you choose to call us enemies of the human race, rather than of human error. Nay, who would deliver you from those secret foes, ever busy both destroying your souls and ruining your health? Who would save you, I mean, from the attacks of those spirits of evil, which without reward or hire we exorcise? This alone would be revenge enough for us, that you were henceforth left free to the possession of unclean spirits. But instead of taking into account what is due to us for the important protection we afford you, and though we are not merely no trouble to you, but in fact necessary to your well-being, you prefer to hold us enemies, as indeed we are, yet not of man, but rather of his error.

Chapter Fifty

In that case, you say, why do you complain of our persecutions? You ought rather to be grateful to us for giving you the sufferings you want. Well, it is quite true that it is our desire to suffer, but it is in the way that the soldier longs for war. No one indeed suffers willingly, since suffering necessarily implies fear and danger. Yet the man who objected to the conflict, both fights with all his strength, and when victorious, he rejoices in the battle, because he reaps from it glory and spoil. It is our battle to be summoned to your tribunals that there, under fear of execution, we may battle for the truth. But the day is won when the object of the struggle is gained. This victory of ours gives us the glory of pleasing God, and the spoil of life eternal. But we are overcome. Yes, when we have obtained our wishes. Therefore we conquer in dying; we go forth victorious at the very time we are subdued. . . . This is the attitude in which we conquer, it is our victory-robe, it is for us a sort of triumphal car. Naturally enough, therefore, we do not please the vanquished; on account of this, indeed, we are counted a desperate, reckless race. But the very desperation and recklessness you object to in us, among yourselves lift high the standard of virtue in the cause of glory and of fame. . . . O glory legitimate, because it is human, for whose sake it is counted neither reckless foolhardiness, nor desperate obstinacy, to despise death itself and all sorts of savage treatment; for whose sake you may for your native place, for the empire, for friendship, endure all you are forbidden to do for God! And you cast statues in honor of persons such as these, and you put inscriptions upon images, and cut out epitaphs on tombs, that their names may never perish. In so far as you can by your monuments, you yourselves afford a son of resurrection to the dead. Yet he who expects the true resurrection from God is insane, if for God he suffers! But go zealously on, good presidents, you will stand higher with the people if you sacrifice the Christians at their wish, kill us, torture us, condemn us, grind us to dust; your injustice is the proof that we are innocent. Therefore God suffers that we thus suffer; for but very lately, in condemning a Christian woman to the leno rather than to the leo you made confession that a taint on our purity is considered among us something more terrible than any punishment and any death. Nor does your cruelty, however exquisite, avail you; it is rather a temptation to us. The more we are mown down by you, the more in number we grow; the blood of Christians is seed. Many of your writers exhort to the courageous bearing of pain and death, as Cicero in the Tusculans, as Seneca in his Chances, as Diogenes, Pyrrhus, Callinicus; and yet their words do not find so many disciples as Christians do, teachers not by words, but by their deeds. That very obstinacy you rail against is the precept. For who that contemplates it is not excited to inquire what is at the bottom of it? Who, after inquiry, does not embrace our doctrines? Then, when he has embraced them, who does not desire to suffer that he may become partaker of the fullness of God's grace, that he may obtain from God complete forgiveness, by giving in exchange his blood? For that secures the remission of all offences. On this account it is that we return thanks on the very spot for your sentences. As the divine and human are ever opposed to each other, when we are condemned by you, we are acquitted by the Highest.

ANF 3, ed. A. Cleveland Coxe. Reprint, Peabody, MA: Hendrickson, 1994.

Tertullian of Carthage (160–212)
To Scapula

Scapula was the acting ruler of the province, and Tertullian wrote this letter attempting to dissuade him from continuing the persecution. There is almost a sense of desire for martyrdom in this selection, calling it "our glory." The emphasis, though, is not on the individual rewards to the martyr, but the rewards to those who become Christians through the witness of the martyr. Regardless of the number of believers killed, the community of faith would persist through its constant growth.

Chapter Five

Your cruelty is our glory. Only see you to it, that in having such things as these to endure, we do not feel ourselves constrained to rush forth to the combat, if only to prove that we have no dread of them, but on the contrary, even invite their infliction. . . . How many fires, how many swords will be required? What will be the anguish of Carthage itself, which you will have to decimate, as each one recognizes there his relatives and companions, as he sees there it may be men of your own order, and noble ladies, and all the leading persons of the city, and either kinsmen or friends of those of your own circle? Spare yourself, if not us poor Christians! Spare Carthage, if not yourself! Spare the province, which the indication of your purpose has subjected to the threats and extortions at once of the soldiers and of private enemies. We have no master but God. He is before you, and cannot be hidden from you, but to him you can do no injury. But those whom you regard as masters are only men, and one day they themselves must die. Yet still this community will be undying, for be assured that just in the time of its seeming overthrow it is built up into greater power. For all who witness the noble patience of its martyrs, as struck with misgivings, are inflamed with desire to examine into the matter in question; and as soon as they come to know the truth, they immediately enroll themselves its disciples.

ANF 3, ed. A. Cleveland Coxe. Reprint, Peabody, MA: Hendrickson, 1994.

Origen of Alexandria (185–254)

Against Celsus

Celsus was a second century pagan philosopher whose only known work, *True Doctrine,* was an attack on Christianity. His central objection was to the exclusive claim of the church to possess the message of God, though he also found the doctrines of the Incarnation and Resurrection of Christ to be absurd. He believed that Jesus had been a magician, trained in the Egyptian arts, and remarked that faith, rather than rationalism, was the religion only of women, children, and slaves. In response to Celsus' interpretation of Christianity, third-century Alexandrian teacher Origen wrote the lengthy treatise from which the following selections are drawn.

In Book One Origen denied the charge that Christians held their teachings secretly rather than publicly. He responded that there was no place where people were unaware of the doctrine of the Christian faith because the church had shared its message with everyone, everywhere. Celsus also had charged that Christianity was an irrational religion. Origen argued that while most might not have investigated for themselves what the teachings of the faith were, the teachers in the church had explained them. He said this was analogous to a sick patient trusting the prognosis of a physician even if the patient had no medical training. Third, Origen remarked that all socioeconomic classes were represented in the community, and no groups of people were unwelcome. Finally, he explained that Jesus chose ignorant and sinful people to be his followers precisely because he could demonstrate his power by changing them into preachers of his message.

The selections from Book Three were written in response to the accusation that Christians did not want to allow others into their community. Celsus had argued that when the church was small there was little dissent, but as it grew the members split in order to maintain control over their group. Origen said this was baseless. He pointed out that believers longed for the conversion of others, and to that end shared the message of Christ with all peoples everywhere. He stated that they desired for everyone to enter into fellowship with God. Unlike the philosophers, who simply shared their message with any who would stop and listen, the Christians took time to instruct those who were interested until they understood Christianity and agreed to abide in it. Then these converts would join the community. The church, then, did not exist solely for itself, but for the conversion of other people.

Origen referred to Christians as ambassadors of truth in Book Six. Their responsibility was to win the multitudes from every class, race, and region to their faith by proclamation of the message of Christ. He offered Scripture as an example, citing the manner in which it employed simple language in order to reach everyone and not simply the educated. Christian evangelism was not intended to impress its hearers with style and rhetoric, but to see them changed from those who were wicked to those who were good. Finally, in Book Seven, Origen articulated the same interpretation as Tertullian about persecution: it aided the expansion of the Christian community.

Book One, Chapter Seven

Moreover, since he frequently calls the Christian doctrine a secret system of belief, we must confute him on this point also, since almost the entire world is better acquainted with what Christians preach than with the favorite opinions of philosophers. For who is ignorant of the statement that Jesus was born of a virgin, and that he was crucified, and that his resurrection is an article of faith among many, and that a general judgment is announced to come, in which the wicked are to be punished according to their deserts, and the righteous to be duly rewarded? And yet the mystery of the resurrection, not being understood, is made a subject of ridicule among unbelievers. In these circumstances, to speak of the Christian doctrine as a secret system is altogether absurd. But that there should be certain doctrines, not made known to the multitude, which are revealed after the exoteric ones have been taught, is not a peculiarity of Christianity alone, but also of philosophic systems, in which certain truths are exoteric and others esoteric. Some of the hearers of Pythagoras were content with his very own words; while others were taught in secret those doctrines which were not deemed fit to be communicated to profane and insufficiently prepared ears. Moreover, all the mysteries that are celebrated everywhere throughout Greece and barbarous countries, although held in secret, have no discredit thrown upon them, so that it is in vain that he endeavors to calumniate the secret doctrines of Christianity, seeing he does not correctly understand its nature.

Chapter Nine

He next proceeds to recommend, that in adopting opinions we should follow reason and a rational guide, since he who assents to opinions without following this course is very liable to be deceived. . . . For as among such persons are frequently to be found wicked men, who, taking advantage of the ignorance of those who are easily deceived, lead them away whither they will, so also, he says, is the case among Christians. And he asserts that certain persons who do not wish either to give or receive a reason for their belief, keep repeating, "Do not examine, but believe!" and, "Your faith will save you!" And he alleges that such also say, "The wisdom of this life is bad, but that foolishness is a good thing!" To which we have to answer, that if it were possible for all to leave the business of life, and devote themselves to philosophy, no other method ought to be adopted by any one, but this alone. For in the Christian system also it will be found that there is, not to speak at all arrogantly, at least as much of investigation into articles of belief, and of explanation of dark sayings, occurring in the prophetical writings, and of the parables in the Gospels, and of countless other things, which either were narrated or enacted with a symbolical signification—as is the case with other systems. But since the course alluded to is impossible, partly on account of the necessities of life, partly on account of the weakness of men, as only a very few individuals devote themselves earnestly to study, what better method could be devised with a view of assisting the multitude, than that which was delivered by Jesus to the heathen? And let us inquire, with respect to the great multitude of believers, who have washed away the mire of wickedness in which they formerly wallowed, whether it were better for them to believe without a reason, and so to have become reformed and improved in their habits, through the belief that men are chastised for sins, and honored for good works or not to have allowed themselves to be converted on the strength of mere faith, but have waited until they could give themselves to a thorough examination of the necessary reasons. For it is manifest that, with such a plan, all men, with very few exceptions, would not obtain this amelioration of conduct which they have obtained through a simple faith, but would continue to remain in the practice of a wicked life. Now, whatever other evidence can be furnished of the fact, that it was not without divine intervention that the philanthropic scheme of Christianity was introduced among men, this also must be added. For a pious man will not believe that even a physician of the body, who restores the sick to better health, could take up his abode in any city or country without divine permission, since no good happens to men without the help of God. And if he who has cured the bodies of many, or restored them to better health, does not effect his cures without the help of God, how much more he who has healed the souls of many, and has turned them to virtue, and improved their nature, and attached them to God who is over all things, and taught them to refer every action to his good pleasure, and to shun all that is displeasing to him, even to the least of their words or deeds, or even of the thoughts of their hearts?

Chapter Twenty-Seven

Any one who examines the subject will see that Jesus attempted and successfully accomplished works beyond the reach of human power. For although, from the very beginning, all things opposed the spread of his doctrine in the world, both the princes of the times, and their chief captains and generals, and all, to speak generally, who were possessed of the smallest influence, and in addition to these, the rulers of the different cities, and the soldiers, and the people, yet it proved victorious, as being the Word of God, the nature of which is such that it cannot be hindered; and becoming more powerful than all such adversaries, it made itself master of the whole of Greece, and a considerable portion of Barbarian lands, and convened countless numbers of souls to his religion. And although, among the multitude of converts to Christianity, the simple and ignorant necessarily outnumbered the more intelligent, as the former class always does the latter, yet Celsus, unwilling to take note of this, thinks that this philanthropic doctrine, which reaches to every soul under the sun, is vulgar, and on account of its vulgarity and its want of reasoning power, obtained a hold only over the ignorant. And yet he himself admits that it was not the simple alone who were led by the doctrine of Jesus to adopt his religion; for he acknowledges that there were among them some persons of moderate intelligence, and gentle disposition, and possessed of understanding, and capable of comprehending allegories.

Chapter Sixty-Three

And since Celsus has termed the apostles of Jesus men of infamous notoriety, saying that they were tax-gatherers and sailors of the vilest character, we have to remark, with respect to this charge, that he seems, in order to bring an accusation against Christianity, to believe the Gospel accounts only where he pleases, and to express his disbelief of them, in order that he may not be forced to admit the manifestations of Divinity related in these same books; whereas one who sees the spirit of truth by which the writers are influenced, ought, from their narration of things of inferior importance, to believe also the account of divine things. Now in the general Letter of Barnabas, from which perhaps Celsus took the statement that the apostles were notoriously wicked men, it is recorded that "Jesus selected his own apostles, as persons who were more guilty of sin than all other evildoers." And in the Gospel according to Luke, Peter says to Jesus, "Depart from me, O Lord, for I am a sinful man." Moreover, Paul, who himself also at a later time became an apostle of Jesus, says in his Letter to Timothy, "This is a faithful saying, that Jesus Christ came into the world to save sinners, of whom I am the chief." And I do not know how Celsus should have forgotten or not have thought of saying something about Paul, the founder, after Jesus, of the Churches that are in Christ. He saw, probably, that anything he might say about that apostle would require to be explained, in consistency with the fact that, after being a persecutor of the Church of God, and a bitter opponent of believers, who went so far even as to deliver over the disciples of Jesus to death, so great a change afterwards passed over him, that he preached the Gospel of Jesus from Jerusalem round about to Illyricum, and was ambitious to carry the glad tidings where he needed not to build upon another man's foundation, but to places where the Gospel of God in Christ had not been proclaimed at all. What absurdity, therefore, is there, if Jesus, desiring to manifest to the human race the power which he possesses to heal souls, should have selected notorious and wicked men, and should have raised them to such a degree of moral excellence, that they, became a pattern of the purest virtue to all who were converted by their instrumentality to the Gospel of Christ?

Book Three, Chapter Nine

But since he is manifestly guilty of falsehood in the statements which follow, let us examine his assertion when he says, "If all men wished to become Christians, the latter would not desire such a result." Now that the above statement is false is clear from this, that Christians do not neglect, as far as in them lies, to take measures to disseminate their doctrine throughout the whole world. Some of them, accordingly, have made it their business to itinerate not only through cities, but even villages and country houses, that they might make converts to God. And no one would maintain that they did this for the sake of gain, when sometimes they would not accept even necessary sustenance; or if at any time they were pressed by a necessity of this sort, were contented with the mere supply of their wants, although many were willing to share their abundance with them, and to bestow help upon them far above their need. At the present day, indeed, when, owing to the multitude of Christian believers, not only rich men, but persons of rank, and delicate and high-born ladies, receive the teachers of Christianity, some perhaps will dare to say that it is for the sake of a little glory that certain individuals assume the office of Christian instructors. It is impossible, however, rationally to entertain such a suspicion with respect to Christianity in its beginnings, when the danger incurred, especially by its teachers, was great; while at the present day the discredit attaching to it among the rest of mankind is greater than any supposed honor enjoyed among those who hold the same belief, especially when such honor is not shared by all. It is false, then, from the very nature of the case, to say that "if all men wished to become Christians, the latter would not desire such a result."

Chapter Ten

But observe what he alleges as a proof of his statement: "Christians at first were few in number, and held the same opinions; but when they grew to be a great multitude, they were divided and separated, each wishing to have his own individual party: for this was their object from the beginning." That Christians at first were few in number, in comparison with the multitudes who subsequently became Christian, is undoubted; and yet, all things considered, they were not so very few. For what stirred up the envy of the Jews against Jesus, and aroused them to conspire against him, was the great number of those who followed him into the wilderness, five thousand men on one occasion, and four thousand on another, having attended him thither, without including the women and children. For such was the charm of Jesus' words, that not only were men willing to follow him to the wilderness, but women also, forgetting the weakness of their sex and a regard for outward propriety in thus following their Teacher into desert places. Children, too, who are altogether unaffected by such emotions, either following their parents, or perhaps attracted also by his divinity, in order that it might be implanted within them, became his followers along with their parents. But let it be granted that Christians were few in number at the beginning, how does that help to prove that Christians would be unwilling to make all men believe the doctrine of the Gospel?

Chapter Fifty-One

And if they are not to be blamed for so doing, let us see whether Christians do not exhort multitudes to the practice of virtue in a greater and better degree than they. For the philosophers who converse in public do not pick and choose their hearers, but he who likes stands and listens. The Christians, however, having previously, so far as possible, tested the souls of those who wish to become their hearers, and having previously instructed them in private, when they appear before entering the community to have sufficiently evinced their desire towards a virtuous life, introduce them then, and not before, privately forming one class of those who are beginners, and are receiving admission, but who have not yet obtained the mark of complete purification; and another of those who have manifested to the best of their ability their intention to desire no other things than are approved by Christians; and among these there are certain persons appointed to make inquiries regarding the lives and behavior of those who join them, in order that they may prevent those who commit acts of infamy from coming into their public assembly, while those of a different character they receive with their whole heart, in order that they may daily make them better. And this is their method of procedure, both with those who are sinners, and especially with those who lead dissolute lives, whom they exclude from their community, although, according to Celsus, they resemble those who in the market-places perform the most shameful tricks.

Chapter Fifty-Four

We acknowledge, however, although Celsus will not have it so, that we do desire to instruct all men in the word of God, so as to give to young men the exhortations which are appropriate to them, and to show to slaves how they may recover freedom of thought, and be ennobled by the word. And those among us who are the ambassadors of Christianity sufficiently declare that they are debtors to Greeks and Barbarians, to wise men and fools, for they do not deny their obligation to cure the souls even of foolish persons, in order that as far as possible they may lay aside their ignorance, and endeavor to obtain greater prudence, by listening also to the words of Solomon: "Oh, fools, have an understanding heart," and "Who is the most simple among you, let him turn unto me"; and wisdom exhorts those who are devoid of understanding in the words, "Come, eat of my bread, and drink of the wine which I have mixed for you. Forsake folly that you may live, and correct understanding in knowledge." This too would I say, seeing it bears on the point, in answer to the statement of Celsus: Do not philosophers invite young men to their lectures? and do they not encourage young men to exchange a wicked life for a better? and do they not desire slaves to learn philosophy? Must we find fault, then, with philosophers who have exhorted slaves to the practice of virtue? . . . Is it indeed permissible for you, O Greeks, to call youths and slaves and foolish persons to the study of philosophy, but if we do so, we do not act from philanthropic motives in wishing to heal every rational nature with the medicine of reason, and to bring them into fellowship with God, the Creator of all things? These remarks, then, may suffice in answer to what are slanders rather than accusations on the part of Celsus.

Chapter Sixty-Eight

That philosophical discourses, however, distinguished by orderly arrangement and elegant expression, should produce such results in the case of those individuals just enumerated, and upon others who have led wicked lives, is not at all to be wondered at. But when we consider that those discourses, which Celsus terms "vulgar," are filled with power, as if they were spells, and see that they at once convert multitudes from a life of licentiousness to one of extreme regularity, and from a life of wickedness to a better, and from a state of cowardice or unmanliness to one of such high-toned courage as to lead men to despise even death through the piety which shows itself within them, why should we not justly admire the power which they contain? For the words of those who at the first assumed the office of Christian ambassadors, and who gave their labors to rear up the Churches of God, nay, their preaching also, were accompanied with a persuasive power, though not like that found among those who profess the philosophy of Plato, or of any other merely human philosopher, which possesses no other qualities than those of human nature. But the demonstration which followed the words of the apostles of Jesus was given from God, and was accredited us by the Spirit and by power. And therefore their word ran swiftly and speedily, or rather the word of God through their instrumentality, transformed numbers of persons who had been sinners both by nature and habit, whom no one could have reformed by punishment, but who were changed by the word, which molded and transformed them according to its pleasure.

Book Six, Chapter One

We maintain, that if it is the object of the ambassadors of the truth to confer benefits upon the greatest possible number, and, so far as they can, to win over to its side, through their love to men, every one without exception—intelligent as well as simple—not Greeks only, but also Barbarians—and great, indeed, is the humanity which should succeed in converting the rustic and the ignorant. It is manifest that they must adopt a style of address fitted to do good to all, and to gain over to them men of every sort. Those, on the other hand, who turn away from the ignorant as being mere slaves, and unable to understand the flowing periods of a polished and logical discourse, and so devote their attention solely to such as have been brought up among literary pursuits, confine their views of the public good within very strait and narrow limits.

Chapter Two

I have made these remarks in reply to the charges which Celsus and others bring against the simplicity of the language of Scripture, which appears to be thrown into the shade by the splendor of polished discourse. For our prophets, and Jesus Himself, and his apostles, were careful to adopt a style of address which should not merely convey the truth, but which should be fitted to gain over the multitude, until each one, attracted and led onwards, should ascend as far as he could towards the comprehension of those mysteries which are contained in these apparently simple words. For, if I may venture to say so, few have been benefited (if they have indeed been benefited at all) by the beautiful and polished style of Plato, and those who have written like him; while, on the contrary, many have received advantage from those who wrote and taught in a simple and practical manner, and with a view to the wants of the multitude. It is easy, indeed, to observe that Plato is found only in the hands of those who profess to be literary men; while Epictetus is admired by persons of ordinary capacity, who have a desire to be benefited, and who perceive the improvement which may be derived from his writings. Now we make these remarks, not to disparage Plato (for the great world of men has found even him useful), but to point out the aim of those who said: "And my speech and my preaching was not with enticing words of man's wisdom, but in demonstration of the Spirit and of power, that our faith should not stand in the wisdom of men, but in the power of God." For the word of God declares that the preaching (although in itself true and most worthy of belief) is not sufficient to reach the human heart, unless a certain power be imparted to the speaker from God, and a grace appear upon his words; and it is only by the divine agency that this takes place in those who speak effectually. The prophet says in the sixty-seventh Psalm, that "the Lord will give a word with great power to them who preach." If, then, it should be granted with respect to certain points, that the same doctrines are found among the Greeks as in our own Scriptures, yet they do not possess the same power of attracting and disposing the souls of men to follow them. And therefore the disciples of Jesus, men ignorant so far as regards Grecian philosophy, yet traversed many countries of the world, impressing, agreeably to the desire of the Logos, each one of their hearers according to his deserts, so that they received a moral amelioration in proportion to the inclination of their will to accept of that which is good.

Book Seven, Chapter Twenty-Six

[The providence of God] has extended day by day the Christian religion, so that it is now preached everywhere with boldness, and that in spite of the numerous obstacles which oppose the spread of Christ's teaching in the world. But since it was the purpose of God that the nations should receive the benefits of Christ's teaching, all the devices of men against Christians have been brought to naught; for the more that kings, and rulers, and peoples have persecuted them everywhere, the more have they increased in number and grown in strength.

ANF 4, ed. A. Cleveland Coxe. Reprint, Peabody, MA: Hendrickson, 1994.

John Chrysostom of Constantinople (347–407)
Homily 3 on 1 Corinthians

In this sermon, John the "Golden-tongued" explained that unbelievers would not have been won to the Christian community through eloquent speaking, but through right living. One finds this theme running through each of these selections. "Let us win them by our life," he exhorted his audience. Proclamation of the message of Christ should have been accompanied by a lifestyle reflective of the faith. He also instructed his hearers to share the teachings of Christianity with all people, though perhaps only a few would have responded. The fact that few people would respond should not have been a discouragement, for, John said, one must be faithful in the little to obtain the large.

"Not in wisdom of words, lest the Cross of Christ should be made of no effect."

Having brought down the swelling pride of those who were arrogant because of their baptizing [previously in the sermon], he changes his ground afterwards to meet those who boasted about heathen wisdom, and against them he puts on his armor with more vehemence. For to those who were puffed up with baptizing he said, "I give thanks that I baptized no one"; and, "for Christ sent me not to baptize." He speaks neither vehemently nor argumentatively, but, having just hinted his meaning in a few words, passes on quickly. But here at the very outset he gives a severe blow, saying, "Lest the Cross of Christ be made void." Why then pride yourself on a thing which ought to make you hide your face? Since, if this wisdom is at war with the Cross and fights with the Gospel, it is not meet to boast about it, but to retire with shame. For this was the cause why the Apostles were not wise; not through any weakness of the Gift, but lest the Gospel preached suffer harm. The sort of people therefore above mentioned were not those employed in advocating the Word: rather they were among its defamers. The unlearned men were the establishers of it. This was able to check vainglory, this to repress arrogance, this to enforce moderation.

"But if it was 'not by wisdom of speech,' why did they send Apollos who was eloquent?" It was not, he replies, through confidence in his power of speech, but because he was "mighty in the Scriptures," and "confuted the Jews." And besides the point in question was that the leaders and first disseminators of the word were not eloquent; since these were the very persons to require some great power, for the expulsion of error in the first instance; and then, namely at the very outset, was the abundant strength needed. Now he who could do without educated persons at first, if afterwards some being eloquent were admitted by him, he did so not because he wanted them, but because he would make no distinctions. For as he needed not wise men to effect whatever he would, so neither, if any were afterwards found such, did he reject them on that account.

8. But prove to me that Peter and Paul were eloquent. You can not: for they were "unlearned and ignorant men"! As therefore Christ, when he was sending out his disciples into the world, having shown unto them his power in Palestine first, and said, "When I sent you forth without purse and wallet and shoe, lacked you any thing?" permitted them from that time forward to possess both a wallet and a purse; so also he has done here: for the point was the manifestation of Christ's power, not the rejection of persons from the Faith on account of their Gentile wisdom, if they were drawing near. When the Greeks then charge the disciples with being uneducated, let us be even more forward in the charge than they. Nor let anyone say, "Paul was wise"; but while we exalt those among them who were great in wisdom and admired for their excellency of speech, let us allow that all on our side were uneducated; for it will be no slight overthrow which they will sustain from us in that respect also: and so the victory will be brilliant indeed.

I have said these things, because I once heard a Christian disputing in a ridiculous manner with a Greek, and both parties in their mutual fray ruining themselves. For what things the Christian ought to have said, these the Greek asserted; and what things it was natural to expect the Greek would say, these the Christian pleaded for himself. As thus: the dispute being about Paul and Plato, the Greek endeavored to show that Paul was unlearned and ignorant; but the Christian, from simplicity, was anxious to prove that Paul was more eloquent than Plato. And so the victory was on the side of the Greek, this argument being allowed to prevail. For if Paul was a more considerable person than Plato, many probably would object that it was not by grace, but by excellency of speech that he prevailed; so that the Christian's assertion made for the Greek. And what the Greek said made wisdom, but of the grace of God.

Therefore, lest we fall into the same error, and be laughed to scorn, arguing thus with Greeks whenever we have a controversy with them; let us charge the Apostles with want of learning; for this same charge is praise. And when they say that the Apostles were rude, let us follow up the remark and say that they were also untaught, and unlettered, and poor, and vile, and stupid, and obscure. It is not a slander on the Apostles to say so, but it is even a glory that, being such, they should have outshone the whole world. For these untrained, and rude, and illiterate men, as completely vanquished the wise, and powerful, and the tyrants, and those who flourished in wealth and glory and all outward good things, as though they had not been men at all: from whence it manifest that great is the power of the Cross; and that these things were done by no human strength. For the results do not keep the course of nature, rather what was done was above all nature. Now when any thing takes place above nature, and exceedingly above it, on the side of rectitude and utility; it is quite plain that these things are done by some Divine power and cooperation. And observe; the fisherman, the tentmaker, the publican, the ignorant, the unlettered, coming from the far distant country of Palestine, and having beaten off their own ground the philosophers, the masters of oratory, the skillful debaters alone prevailed against them in a short space of time; in the midst of many perils; the opposition of peoples and kings, the striving of nature herself, length of time, the vehement resistance of inveterate custom, demons in arms, the devil in battle array and stirring up all, kings, rulers, peoples, nations, cities, barbarians, Greeks, philosophers, orators, sophists, historians, laws, tribunals, divers kinds of punishments, deaths innumerable and of all sorts. But nevertheless all these were confuted and gave way when the fisherman spoke; just like the light dust which cannot bear the rush of violent winds. Now what I say is, let us learn thus to dispute with the Greeks; that we be not like beasts and cattle, but prepared concerning "the hope which is in us." And let us pause for a while to work out this topic, no unimportant bare naked body they overthrew all their foes using no weapons but striking with the hand, and in conclusion killed some, and others took captive and led away, themselves receiving not so much as a wound; would anyone have ever said that the thing was of man? And yet the trophy of the Apostles is much more wonderful than that. For a naked man's escaping a wound is not so wonderful by far as that the ordinary and unlettered person—that a fisherman—should overcome such a degree of talent: and neither for fewness, nor for poverty, nor for dangers, nor for prepossession of habit, nor for so great austerity of the precepts enjoined, nor for the daily deaths, nor for the multitude of those who were deceived nor for the great reputation of the deceivers be turned from his purpose.

9. Let us overcome by our manner of living rather than by our words alone. For this is the main battle, this is the unanswerable arguments the argument from conduct. For though we give ten thousand precepts of philosophy in words, if we do not exhibit a life better than theirs, the gain is nothing. For it is not what is said that draws their attention, but their enquiry is, what we do; and they say, "Do you first obey your own words, and then admonish others." But if while you say, infinite are the blessings in the world to come, you seem yourself to be nailed down to this world, just as if no such things existed, when you weep immoderately over the departed, then you reverse it often in their minds. And this is what keeps the unbelievers from becoming Christians.

Let us win them therefore by our life. Many, even among the untaught, have in that way astounded the minds of philosophers, as having exhibited in themselves also that philosophy which lies in deeds, and uttered a voice clearer than a trumpet by their mode of life and self-denial. For this is stronger than the tongue. But when I say, "One ought not to bear malice," and then do all manner of evils to the Greek, how shall I be able by words to win him, while by my deeds I am frightening him away? Let us catch them then by our mode of life; and by these souls let us build up the Church, and of these let us amass our wealth. There is nothing to weigh against a soul, not even the whole world. So that although you give countless treasure unto the poor, you will do no such work as he who converted one soul. "For he that takes forth the precious from the vile shall be as my mouth": so he speaks. A great good it is, I grant, to have pity on the poor; but it is nothing equal to the withdrawing them from error. For he that does this resembles Paul and Peter: we being permitted to take up their Gospel, not with perils such as theirs; with endurance of famines and pestilences, and all other evils—for the present is a season of peace—but so as to display that diligence which comes from zeal. For even while we sit at home we may practice this kind of fishery. Who has a friend or relation or inmate of his house, these things let him say, these do; and he shall be like Peter and Paul. And why do I say Peter and Paul? he shall be the mouth of Christ. For he said, "He that takes forth the precious from the vile shall be as my mouth." And though you persuade not today, tomorrow you shall persuade. And though you never persuade, you shall have your own reward in full. And though you persuade not all, a few out of many persuade all men; but still they discoursed with all, and for all they have their reward. For not according to the result of the things that are well done, but according to the intention of the doers, is God wont to assign the crowns; though you pay down but two farthings, he receives them; and what he did in the case of the widow, the same will he do also in the case of those who teach. Do not you then, because you can not save the world, despise the few; nor through longing after great things, withdraw yourself from the lesser. If you can not a hundred, take charge of ten; if you can not ten, despise not even five; if you can not five, do not overlook one; and if you can not one, neither so despair, nor keep back what may be done by you. Do you not see how, in matters of trade, they who are so employed make their profit not only of gold but of silver also? For if we do not flight the little things, we shall keep hold also of the great. But if we despise the small, neither shall we easily lay hand upon the other. Thus individuals become rich, gathering both small things and great. And so let us act; that in all things enriched, we may obtain the kingdom of heaven; through the grace and loving-kindness of our Lord Jesus Christ, through whom and with whom unto the Father together with the Holy Spirit be glory, power, honor, now and henceforth and for evermore. Amen.

NPNF 1.12, ed. Philip Schaff. Reprint, Peabody, MA: Hendrickson, 1994.

John Chrysostom of Constantinople (347–407)
Homily 5 on 1 Corinthians

John used this sermon to intimate the source of genuine conversions to Christianity: divine power. He illustrated this by pointing out that Jesus' disciples were effective in their evangelism only because they had witnessed his resurrection from the dead. Nothing else, he argued, would have explained their dramatic conversions. This same divine power would enable his hearers to do the same thing. His audience's employment would not have hindered them because the Apostle Paul was employed but saw many converts.

Tell me then, what were the enticing arguments whereupon they acted, when about to take hold of the Gospel, and to go forth unto all the world? Was there any kind of impediment wanting to restrain them? If they had been mad (for I will not cease repeating it), they could not have succeeded at all; for no one follows the advice of madmen. But if they succeeded as in truth they did succeed, and the event proves, then none so wise as they. Now if none were so wise as they, it is quite plain, they would not lightly have entered upon the preaching. Had they not seen him after he was risen, what was there sufficient to draw them out unto this war? What which would not have turned them away from it? He said unto them, "After three days I will rise again," and he made promises concerning the kingdom of heaven. He said, they should master the whole world, after they had received the Holy Spirit; and ten thousand other things besides these, surpassing all nature. So that if none of these things had come to pass, although they believed in him while alive, after his death they would not have believed in him, unless they had seen him after he was risen. For they have said, "'After three days,' he said, 'I will rise again,' and he has not arisen. He promised that he would give the Spirit, and he has not sent him. How then shall his sayings about the other world find credit with us, when his sayings about this are tried and found wanting?"

And why, if he rose not again, did they preach that he was risen? "Because they loved him," you will say. But surely, it was likely that they would hate him afterwards, for deceiving and betraying them; and because, having lifted them up with innumerable hopes, and divorced them from house, and parents, and all things, and set in hostility against them the entire nation of Jews, he had betrayed them after all. And if indeed the thing were of weakness, they might have pardoned it; but now it would be deemed a result of exceeding malice. For he ought to have spoken the truth, and not have promised heaven, being a mortal man, as you say. So that the very opposite was the likely line for them to take; to proclaim the deception, and declare him a pretender and imposter. Thus again would they have been rid of all their perils; thus have put an end to the war. Moreover, seeing that the Jews gave money unto the sails to say that they stole the body, if the disciples had come forward and said, "We stole him, he is not risen again," what honor would they not have enjoyed? Thus it was in their power to be honored, nay, crowned. Why then did they for insults and dangers barter away these things, if it was not some Divine power which influenced them, and proved mightier than all these?

Now these arguments we ought to practice, not by ourselves only, but one with another; and thus also the discovery of what remains will be easier to us.

11. And do not, because you art an artisan, suppose that this sort of exercise is out of your province; for even Paul was a tent-maker.

"Yes," said some one, "but at that time he was also filled with abundant grace, and out of that he spoke all things" Well; but before this grace, he was at the feet of Gamaliel; yea, moreover, and he received the grace, because of this, that he showed a mind worthy of the grace; and after these things he again put his hand to his craft. Let no one, therefore, of those who have trades be ashamed; but those, who are brought up to nothing and are idle, who employ many attendants, and are served by an immense retinue. For to be supported by continual hard work is a sort of asceticism. The souls of such men are clearer, and their minds better strung. For the man who has nothing to do is more apt to say many things at random, and do many things at random; and he is busy all day long about nothing, a huge lethargy taking him up entirely. But he that is employed will not lightly entertain in himself any thing useless, in deed in words, or in thoughts; for his whole soul is altogether intent upon his laborious way of livelihood. Let us not therefore despise those who support themselves by the labor of their own hands; but let us rather call them happy on this account. For tell me, what thanks are due unto you, when after having received your portion from your father, you go on not in any calling, but lavishing away the whole of it at random? Do you not know that we shall not all have enjoyed greater license here a more exact one; those who were afflicted with labor, or poverty, or any thing else of this kind, one not so severe? And this is plain from Lazarus and the rich man. For as you, for neglecting the right use of the leisure, art justly accused; so the poor man, who having full employment has spent his remnant of time upon right objects, great will be the crowns which he shall receive. But dost you urge that a soldier's duties should at least excuse you; and dost you charge them with your want of leisure? The excuse cannot be founded in reason. For Cornelius was a centurion, yet in no way did the soldier's belt impair his strict rule of life. But you, when you art keeping holiday with dancers and players, and making entire waste of your life upon the stage, never think of excusing yourself from such engagements by the necessity of military service or the fear of rulers: but when it is the Church to which we call you, then occur these endless impediments.

And what will you say in the day, when you see the flame, and the rivers of fire, and the chains never to be broken; and shall hear the gnashing of teeth? Who shall stand up for you in that day, when you shall see him that has labored with his own hand and has lived uprightly, enjoying all glory; but yourself, who art now in soft raiment and redolent of perfumes, in incurable woe? What good will your wealth and superfluity do for you? And the artisan—what harm will his poverty do him?

Therefore that we may not suffer then, let us fear what is said now, and let all our time be spent in employment on things which are really indispensable. For so, having propitiated God in regard of our past sins, and adding good deeds for the future, we shall be able to attain unto the kingdom of heaven: through the favor and loving-kindness.

NPNF 1.12, ed. Philip Schaff. Reprint, Peabody, MA: Hendrickson, 1994.

John Chrysostom of Constantinople (347–407)
Homily 6 on 1 Corinthians

In this sermon Chrysostom addressed the question of why miraculous signs were not necessary for validating the Christian message. Signs would not convince wicked persons to turn from their sin, he replied. Rather it would be the right living of Christians that would lead unbelievers to faith in Christ. For this reason, members of the community were instructed to practice moral living and to proclaim the message of Christ to all people.

"And I, brethren, when I came to you, came not with excellency of speech or of wisdom, declaring unto you the testimony of God. For I determined not to know any thing among you, save Jesus Christ, and him crucified."

4. But some one may say perhaps, "If the Gospel is to prevail and has no need of words, lest the Cross be made of none effect; for what reason are signs withheld now?" For what reason? You speak in unbelief and not allowing that they were done even in the times of the Apostles, or dost you truly seek to know? If in unbelief, I will first make my stand against this. I say then, If signs were not done at that time, how did they, chased, and persecuted, and

trembling, and in chains, and having become the common enemies of the world, and exposed to all as a mark for ill usage, and with nothing of their own to allure, neither speech, nor show, nor wealth, nor city, nor nation, nor family, nor pursuit nor glory, nor any such like thing; but with all things contrary, ignorance, meanness, poverty, hatred, enmity, and setting themselves against whole commonwealths, and with such a message to declare; how, I say, did they work conviction? For both the precepts brought much labor, and the doctrines many dangers. And they that heard and were to obey, had been brought up in luxury and drunkenness, and in great wickedness. Tell me then, how did they convince? Where did their credibility come from? For, as I have just said, If without signs they wrought conviction, far greater does the wonder appear. Do not then urge the fact that signs are not done now, as a proof that they were not done then. For as then they were usefully wrought; so now are they no longer so wrought.

Nor does it necessarily follow from discourse being the only instrument of conviction, that now the "preaching" is in "wisdom." For both they who from the beginning sowed the word were unprofessional and unlearned, and spoke nothing of themselves; but what things they received from God, these they distributed to the world: and we ourselves at this time introduce no inventions of our own; but the things which from them we have received, we speak unto all. And not even now persuade we by argumentation; but from the Divine Scriptures and from the miracles done at that time we produce the proof of what we say. On the other hand, even they at that time persuaded not by signs alone, but also by discoursing. And the signs and the testimonies out of the Old Testament, not the cleverness of the things said, made their words appear more powerful.

5. How then, you will say, is it that signs were expedient then, and now inexpedient? Let us suppose a case (for as yet I am contending against the Greek, and therefore I speak hypothetically of what must certainly come to pass), let us, I say, suppose a case; and let the unbeliever consent to believe our affirmations, though it be only by way of concession: for instance, That Christ will come. When then Christ shall come and all the angels with him, and be manifested as God, and all things made subject unto him; will not even the Greek believe? It is quite plain that he will also fall down and worship, and confess him God, though his stubbornness exceed all reckoning. For who, at sight of the heavens opened and him coming upon the clouds, and all the congregation of the powers above spread

around him, and rivers of fire coming on, and all standing by and trembling, will not fall down before him, and believe him God? Tell me, then; shall that adoration and knowledge be accounted unto the Greek for faith? No, on no account. And why not? Because this is not faith. For necessity has done this, and the evidence of the things seen, and it is not of choice, but by the vastness of the spectacle the powers of the mind are dragged along. It follows that by how much the more evident and overpowering the course of events, by so much is the part of faith abridged. For this reason miracles are not done now. . . .

8. Why then do not all believe now? Because things have degenerated: and for this we are to blame. (For from hence the discourse is addressed unto us also.) For surely not even then did they trust to signs alone, but by the mode of life also many of the converts were attracted. For, "Let your light so shine before men," said he, "that they may see your good works, and glorify your Father which is in heaven." And, "They were all of one heart and one soul, neither said any man that aught of the things which he possessed was his own, but they had all things common; and distribution was made unto every man, according as he had need"; and they lived an angelic life. And if the same were done now, we should convert the whole world, even without miracles. But in the meanwhile, let those who will be saved attend to the Scriptures; for they shall find there both these noble doings, and those which are greater than these. For it may be added that the Teachers themselves surpassed the deeds of the others; living in hunger, in thirst, and nakedness. But we are desirous of enjoying great luxury, and rest, and ease; not so they: they cried aloud, "Even unto the present hour we both hunger, and thirst, and are naked, and are buffeted, and have no certain dwelling place. And some ran from Jerusalem unto Illyricum, and another unto the country of the Indians, and another unto that of the Moors, and this to one part of the world, that to another. Whereas we have not the courage to depart even out of our own country; but seek for luxurious living and splendid houses and all other superfluities. For which of us ever was famished for the word of God's sake? Which ever abode in a wilderness? Which ever set out on a distant peregrination? Which of our teachers lived by the labor of his hands to assist others? Which endured death daily? Hence it is that they also who are with us have become slothful. For suppose that one saw soldiers and generals struggling with hunger, and thirst, and death, and with all dreadful things,

and bearing cold and dangers and all like lions, and so prospering; then afterwards, relaxing that strictness, and becoming enervated, and fond of wealth, and addicted to business and bargains, and then overcome by their enemies it were extreme folly to seek for the cause of all this. Now let us reason thus in our own case and that of our ancestors; for we too have become weaker than all, and are nailed down unto this present life.

And if one be found having a vestige of the ancient wisdom, leaving the cities and the market-places, and the society of the world, and the ordering of others, he betakes himself to the mountains: and if one ask the reason of that retirement, he invents a plea which cannot meet with allowance. For, said he, "Lest I perish too, and the edge of my goodness be taken off, I start aside." Now how much better were it for you to become less keen, and to gain others, than abiding on high to neglect your perishing brethren?

When, however, the one sort are careless about virtue, and those who do regard it withdraw themselves far from our ranks, how are we to subdue our enemies? For even if miracles were wrought now, who would be persuaded? Or who of those without would give heed unto us, our iniquity being thus prevalent? For so it is, that our upright living seems unto the many the more trustworthy argument of the two: miracles admitting of a bad construction on the part of obstinate bad men: whereas a pure life will have abundant power to stop the mouth of the devil himself.

9. These things I say, both to governors and governed; and, before all others, unto myself; to the end that the way of life shown forth in us may be truly admirable, that taking our appropriate stations, we may look down on all things present; may despise wealth, and not despise hell; overlook glory, and not overlook salvation; endure toil and labor here, lest we fall into punishment there. Thus let us wage war with the Greeks; thus let us take them captive with a captivity better than liberty.

But while we say these things without intermission, over and over, they occur very seldom. Howbeit, be they done or not, it is right to remind you of them continually. For if some are engaged in deceiving by their fair speech, so much more is it the duty of those who allure back unto the truth, not to grow weary of speaking what is profitable. Again: if the deceivers make use of so many contrivances—spending as they do money, and applying arguments, and undergoing dangers, and making a parade of their patronage—much more should we, who are winning men from deceit, endure both dangers and deaths, and all things; that we may both gain ourselves and others, and become to our enemies irresistible, and so obtain the promised blessings, through the grace and loving-kindness.

NPNF 1.12, ed. Philip Schaff. Reprint, Peabody, MA: Hendrickson, 1994.

John Chrysostom of Constantinople (347–407)
Homily 22 on 1 Corinthians

The sermon that follows explained Paul's statement that he became all things to all people in order to win some. John pointed out that the Apostle's desire to convert everyone to Christianity caused him to identify with his various audiences by putting himself in their particular contexts. This provided an example for Chrysostom to use in his attempt to encourage his hearers to be zealous to win others to Christian faith.

5. Next, having mentioned his servitude, be describes in what follows the various modes of it. . . . And what are these?

Ver. 20. "And I became," says he, "to the Jews as a Jew, that I might gain Jews." And how did this take place? When he was circumcised that he might abolish circumcision. Therefore he said not, "a Jew," but, "as a Jew," which was a wise arrangement. What are you saying? The herald of the world and he who touched the very heavens and shone so bright in grace, does he all at once descend so low? Yea. For this is to ascend. For you are not to look to the fact only of his descending, but also to his raising up him that was bowed down and bringing him up to himself.

"To them that are under the law, as under the law, not being myself under the law, that I might gain them that are under the law." Either it is the explanation of what went before, or he hints at some other thing besides the former: calling those Jews, who were such originally and from the first: but "under the law," the proselytes, or those who became believers and yet adhered to the law. For they were no longer as Jews, yet "under the law." And when was he under the law? When he shaved his head; when he offered sacrifice. Now these things were done, not because his mind changed (since such conduct would have been wickedness), but because his love condescended. For that he might bring over to this faith those who were really Jews, he became such himself not really, showing himself such only, but not such in fact nor doing these things from a mind so disposed. Indeed, how could he, zealous as he was to convert others also, and doing these things only in order that he might free others who did them from that degradation?

Ver. 21. "To them that are without law, as without law." These were neither Jews, nor Christians, nor Greeks; but "outside of the Law," as was Cornelius, and if there were any others like him. For among these also making his appearance, he used to assume many of their ways. But some say that he hints at his discourse with the Athenians from the inscription on the altar, and that so he said, "to them that are without law, as without law."

Then, lest any should think that the matter was a change of mind, he added, "not being without law to God, but under law to Christ"; i.e., "so far from being without law, I am not simply under the Law, but I have that law which is much more exalted than the older one, viz. that of the Spirit and of grace." Therefore also he adds, "to Christ." Then again, having made them confident of his judgment, he states also the gain of such condescension, saying, "that I might gain them that are without law." And every where he brings forward the cause of his condescension, and stops not even here, but says,

Ver. 22. "To the weak became I weak, that I might gain the weak": in this part coming to their case, with a view to which also all these things have been spoken. However, those were much greater things, but this more to the purpose; whence also he has placed it after them. Indeed he did the same thing likewise in his Letter to the Romans, when he was finding fault about meats; and so in many other places.

Next, not to waste time by naming all severally, he said, "I am become all things to all men, that I may by all means save some."

Do you see how far it is carried? "I am become all things to all men," not expecting, however, to save all, but "that I may save though it be but a few." And so great care and service have I undergone, as one naturally would who was about saving all, far however from hoping to gain all: which was truly magnanimous and a proof of burning zeal. Since likewise the sower sowed every where, and saved not all the seed, notwithstanding he did his part. And having mentioned the fewness of those who are saved, again, adding, "by all means," he consoled those to whom this was a grief. For though it be not possible that all the seed should be saved, nevertheless it cannot be that all should perish. Therefore he said, "by all means," because one so ardently zealous must certainly have some success.

NPNF 1.12, ed. Philip Schaff. Reprint, Peabody, MA: Hendrickson, 1994.

John Chrysostom of Constantinople (347–407)

Homily 2 on 2 Thessalonians

In this selection John exhorts his listeners to speak often about hell and the pending judgment of unbelievers. Talk about such a subject was important, John said, in order to serve as a warning to those who will face it if they do not become Christians. While he acknowledged that some might be offended by this type of discussion, he also reminded his congregation that medicine was often distasteful to someone who was ill, but that it ultimately would have led to the person's health.

If the sight only of a dead body so depresses the mind, how much more must hell and the fire unquenchable, how much more the worm that never dies. If we always think of hell, we shall not soon fall into it. For this reason God has threatened punishment; if it was not attended with great advantage to think of it, God would not have threatened it. But because the remembrance of it is able to work great good, for this reason he has put into our souls the terror of it, as a wholesome medicine. Let us not then overlook the great advantage arising from it, but let us continually advert to it, at our dinners, at our suppers. For conversation about pleasant things profits the soul nothing, but renders it more languid, while that about things painful and melancholy cuts off all that is relaxed and dissolute in it, and converts it, and braces it when unnerved. He who converses of theaters and actors does not benefit the soul, but inflames it more, and renders it more careless. He who concerns himself and is busy in other men's matters, often even involves it in dangers by this curiosity. But he who converses about hell incurs no dangers, and renders it more sober.

But dost you fear the offensiveness of such words? Hast you then, if you art silent, extinguished hell? or if you speak of it, have you kindled it? Whether you speak of it or not, the fire boils forth. Let it be continually spoken of, that you may never fall into it. It is not possible that a soul anxious about hell should readily sin. For hear the most excellent advice, "Remember," it says, "your latter end," and you will not sin for ever. A soul that is fearful of giving account cannot but be slow to transgression. For fear being vigorous in the soul does not permit anything worldly to exist in it. For if discourse raised concerning hell so humbles and brings it low, does not the reflection constantly dwelling upon the soul purify it more than any fire?

Let us not remember the kingdom so much as hell. For fear has more power than the promise. And I know that many would despise ten thousand blessings, if they were rid of the punishment, inasmuch as it is even now sufficient for me to escape vengeance, and not to be punished. No one of those who have hell before their eyes will fall into hell. No one of those who despise hell will escape hell. For as among us those who fear the judgment-seats will not be apprehended by them, but those who despise them are chiefly those who fall under them, so it is also in this case. If the Ninevites had not feared destruction, they would have been overthrown, but because they feared, they were not overthrown. If in the time of Noah they had feared the deluge, they would not have been drowned. And if the Sodomites had feared they would not have been consumed by fire. It is a great evil to despise a threat. He who despises threatening will soon experience its reality in the execution of it. Nothing is so profitable as to converse concerning hell. It renders our souls purer than any silver. For hear the prophet saying, "Your judgments are always before me." For although it pains the hearer, it benefits him very much.

For such indeed are all things that profit. For medicines too, and food, at first annoy the sick, and then do him good. And if we cannot bear the severity of words, it is manifest that we shall not be able to bear affliction in very deed. If no one endures a discourse concerning hell, it is evident, that if persecution came on, no one would ever stand firm against fire, against sword. Let us exercise our ears not to be over soft and tender: for from this we shall come to endure even the things themselves. If we be habituated to hear of dreadful things, we shall be habituated also to endure dreadful things. But if we be so relaxed as not to endure even words, when shall we stand against things? Do you see how the blessed Paul despises all things here, and dangers one after another, as not even temptations? Therefore? Because he had been in the practice of despising hell, for the sake of what was God's will. He thought even the experience of hell to be nothing for the sake of the love of Christ; while we do not even endure a discourse concerning it for our own advantage. Now therefore having heard a little, go your ways; but I beseech you if there is any love in you, constantly to revert to discourses concerning these things. They can do you no harm, even if they should not benefit, but assuredly they will benefit you too. For according to our discourses, the soul is qualified. For evil communications, he says, "corrupt good manners." Therefore also good communications improve it; therefore also fearful discourses make it sober. For the soul is a sort of wax. For if you apply cold discourses, you harden and make it callous; but if fiery ones, you melt it; and having melted it, you form it to what you will, and engrave the royal image upon it. Let us therefore stop up our ears to discourses that are vain. It is no little evil; for from it arise all evils.

By these discourses let us regulate as well ourselves as our wives too, our servants, our children, our friends, and, if possible, our enemies. For with these discourses we are able to cut off the greater part of our sins, and it is better to dwell upon things grievous than upon things agreeable, and it is manifest from hence. For, tell me, if you should go into a house where a marriage is celebrated, for a season you are delighted at the spectacle, but afterwards having gone away, you pine with grief that you have not so much. But if you enter the house of mourners, even though they are very rich, when you go away you will be rather refreshed. For there you have not conceived envy, but comfort and consolation in your poverty. You have seen by facts, that riches are no good, poverty no evil, but they are things indifferent. So also now, if you talk about luxury, you the more vex your soul, that is not able perhaps to be luxurious. But if you are speaking against luxury, and introduce discourse concerning hell, the thing will cheer you, and beget much pleasure. For when you consider that luxury will not be able to defend us at all against that fire, you will not seek after it; but if you reflect that it is wont to kindle it even more, you will not only not seek, but will turn from it and reject it.

Let us not avoid discourses concerning hell, that we may avoid hell. Let us not banish the remembrance of punishment, that we may escape punishment. If the rich man had reflected upon that fire, he would not have sinned; but because he never was mindful of it, therefore he fell into it. Tell me, O man, being about to stand before the Judgment-seat of Christ, dost you speak of all things rather than of that? And when you have a matter before a judge, often only relating to words, neither day nor night, at no time or season dost you talk of anything else, but always of that business, and when you art about to give an account of your whole life, and to submit to a trial, can you not bear even with others reminding you of that Judgment? For this reason therefore all things are ruined and undone, because when we are about to stand before a human tribunal concerning matters of this life, we move everything, we solicit all men, we are constantly anxious about it, we do everything for the sake of it: but when we are about, after no long time, to come before the Judgment-seat of Christ, we do nothing either by ourselves, or by others; we do not entreat the Judge. And yet he grants to us a long season of forbearance, and does not snatch us away in the midst of our sins, but permits us to put them off, and that Goodness and Lovingkindness leaves nothing undone of all that belongs to himself. But all is of no avail; on this account the punishment will be the heavier. But God forbid it should be so! Therefore, I beseech you, let us even if but now become watchful. Let us keep hell before our eyes. Let us consider that inexorable Account, that, thinking of those things, we may both avoid vice, and choose virtue, and may be able to obtain the blessings promised to those who love him, by grace and loving-kindness.

NPNF 1.13, ed. Philip Schaff. Reprint, Peabody, MA: Hendrickson, 1994.

ADDITIONAL READINGS

Ferguson, E., ed. *Conversion, Catechumenate, and Baptism in the Early Church*, Studies in Early Christianity, vol 11. New York: Garland, 1993.

Ferguson, E., ed. *Missions and Regional Characteristics of the Early Church*, Studies in Early Christianity, vol 12. New York: Garland, 1993.

Finn, T. M. *From Death to Rebirth: Ritual and Conversion in Antiquity*. New York: Paulist, 1997.

Goodman, M. *Mission and Conversion: Proselytizing in the Religious History of the Roman Empire*. Oxford: Clarendon, 1994.

Green, M. *Evangelism in the Early Church*. London: Hodder and Stoughton, 1970.

Harnack, A. von. *The Mission and Expansion of Christianity in the First Three Centuries*, 2nd ed. New York: Putnam, 1908.

Hinson, E. G. *The Evangelization of the Roman Empire*. Macon, GA: Mercer University Press, 1981.

Kreider, A. *Worship and Evangelism in Pre-Christendom*. Cambridge: Grove, 1995.

Latourette, K. S. *A History of the Expansion of Christianity*. 7 vols. New York: Harper, 1937–1945.

MacMullen, R. *Christianizing the Roman Empire (A.D. 100–400)*. New Haven: Yale University Press, 1984.

Nock, A. D. *Conversion*. Oxford: Clarendon, 1933.

Sider, R. D. *The Gospel and Its Proclamation*. Wilmington, DE: Glazier, 1983.

CHAPTER 6

Leading the Community

Church Officers in the Early Church

ॐ

To ensure that the community functioned properly, the early Christians acknowledged a number of different offices in the church. The number of these leadership positions varied from one congregation to the next, but those who held offices were responsible for the well-being of the community. The needs of the church included instruction in right living, protection from false teachers who might lead the faithful astray, overseeing the proper administration of the sacraments, guiding the assembly in worship, distributing funds to the poor, and ministering to the sick, along with countless other important tasks.

The most prominent offices were those of elder (presbyter) and deacon. Other titles for the first of these offices both in the New Testament and patristic literature were pastor and overseer (bishop). We are told by Jerome that a distinct office of bishop developed in which the elders chose one of their own to be the *primus inter pares,* or "first among equals." Eventually, this distinct role expanded beyond that of pastoring one local community to more of a diocesan framework, in which the bishop exercised authority over a number of churches in a particular region, or diocese. In the extant literature, the offices of elder and bishop were restricted to men.

Even in the New Testament, believers were spoken of as sheep. Elders filled the role of pastors, or shepherds, for the church. They provided spiritual nourishment for the people by expounding to them the Scriptures. They protected the "flock" from infiltration by "wolves" posing as shepherds. Prevailing methods of explaining what Christians were to believe and how they were to live included preaching in corporate worship settings, teaching the catechumens, and offering other times of organized instruction throughout the week. These pastors ensured the unity of the congregation, the orthodoxy of the community, and the safety of the community primarily through their ministry of teaching. For this reason they were held in high regard.

The deacon(ess), from the Greek for a servant, was responsible for assisting the bishops and elders in their various duties. In administering baptism, as we have seen, deacons and deaconesses would help with the initiates. During the Eucharist, they would distribute the elements to the people. Additionally, those in this office distributed the financial resources of the church to those who were in need, particularly widows and orphans.

As the Christian community grew in number, additional offices developed to meet growing needs. Subdeacons assisted the deacons and deaconesses in their many responsibilities. Readers took part in the worship services by reading the Scriptures aloud for the congregation. Widows helped minister to the women in the church.

Qualifications for holding these various positions were quite strict in the patristic writings. Personal character and obedience to Christian morality were of supreme significance in the early church. Candidates were required to meet a number of demands, particularly those found in the Apostle Paul's correspondence to Timothy and Titus in the New Testament concerning leaders. Bishops/presbyters were required to possess theological abilities that demonstrated a knowledge of Scripture. They were expected to have a blameless reputation with those outside the church. The early writers differ on marital concerns: whether a church officer should be married or barred from marriage. Potential officers were to be judged by the entire church as worthy of holding a high post within the church.

Ordination was an act whereby the church publicly acknowledged one's responsibility as a leader in the community. The church saw ordination to be a solemn agreement among the church, the candidate, and God himself. It served to remind the church of an officer's "calling" by God to the position, and to remind the holder of his responsibility to God and to the people. Ordination was not to be taken lightly by either party. Time and again writers dissuaded hasty ordination because those who were immature or untested could too easily fall prey to the temptations associated with great responsibility.

Clement of Rome (Died c. 97)

First Clement

Clement was the Bishop of Rome from 88 to around 97. Some asserted that Clement had been ordained by the Apostle Peter, though he was probably the third or fourth bishop of the Roman church. He is known primarily for his epistle to the church at Corinth, commonly called *First Clement*. In the letter, he reproved the church for deposing the elders, which he also called bishops or overseers, instructing that their authority came from Christ. An anonymous sermon was at one point circulated along with Clement's letter and incorrectly attributed to him. It is still customary to call the sermon *Second Clement*.

In the selections that follow Clement explains that there was a clear order of appointment from God to the leaders of the church at Corinth. He says that God sent Christ, Christ sent the apostles, and the apostles sent overseers and deacons. Those overseers were instructed to appoint successors who would continue the tradition. Clement admonishes the Corinthian Christians for their deposing of faithful leaders.

Clement's use of the terms *bishop/overseer* and *elder* interchangeably is important because the rise of one elder to a status of *primus inter pares* had not yet occurred. He implies that there are two offices in the church, bishop and deacon. While he does not proceed to explain the respective roles of each office, he does indicate that the authority of their position came from God.

Chapter Forty-Two

The apostles have preached the Gospel to us from the Lord Jesus Christ; Jesus Christ has done so from God. Christ therefore was sent forth by God, and the apostles by Christ. Both these appointments, then, were made in an orderly way, according to the will of God. Having therefore received their orders, and being fully assured by the resurrection of our Lord Jesus Christ, and established in the Word of God, with full assurance of the Holy Spirit, they went out proclaiming that the Kingdom of God was at hand. As they were preaching throughout countries and cities, they appointed the first-fruits of their labors, having first proven them by the Spirit, to be bishops and deacons of those who should afterwards believe. This was not a new thing, since indeed many ages before it had been written concerning bishops and deacons. In a certain passage, the Scripture says, "I will appoint their bishops in righteousness, and their deacons in faith."

Chapter Forty-Three

What wonder is it if those in Christ who were entrusted with such a duty by God appointed those ministers mentioned previously [in chapter forty-two], seeing that the blessed Moses, who was "a faithful servant in all his house," noted down in the sacred books all the injunctions which were given him, and that the other prophets followed him, bearing witness with one consent to the ordinances which he had appointed? When rivalry arose concerning the priesthood, and the tribes were contending among themselves as to which of them should be adorned with that glorious title, he commanded the twelve princes of the tribes to bring him their rods, each one being inscribed with the name of the tribe. And he took them and bound them together, and sealed them with the rings of the princes of the tribes, and laid them up in the tabernacle of witness on the table of God. And having shut the doors of the tabernacle, he sealed the keys, as he had done the rods, and said to them, "Men and brethren, the tribe whose rod blossoms God has chosen to fulfill the office of the priesthood, and to minister unto him." The next morning, he assembled all Israel, six hundred thousand men, and showed the seals to the princes of the tribes, and opened the tabernacle of witness, and brought forth the rods. And the rod of Aaron was found not only to have blossomed, but to bear fruit upon it. What do you think, beloved? Did not Moses know beforehand that this would happen? Undoubtedly he knew; but he acted in this way in order that there might be no sedition in Israel, and that the name of the true and only God might be glorified; to whom be glory forever and ever.

Chapter Forty-Four

Our apostles also knew, through our Lord Jesus Christ, that there would be strife on account of the office of the episcopate. For this reason, therefore, inasmuch as they had obtained a perfect fore-knowledge of this, they appointed those ministers already mentioned, and afterwards gave instructions, that when these should die, other approved men should succeed them in their ministry. We are of the opinion, therefore, that those appointed by them, or afterwards by other eminent men, with the consent of the whole Church, and who have blamelessly served the flock of Christ in a humble, peaceable, and disinterested spirit, and have for a long time possessed the good opinion of all, cannot be justly dismissed from the ministry. For our sin will not be small, if we eject from the episcopate those who have blamelessly and holily fulfilled its duties. Blessed are those presbyters who, having finished their course before now, have obtained a fruitful and perfect departure from this world; for they have no fear lest any one deprive them of the place now appointed them. We, however, see that you have removed some men of excellent behavior from the ministry, which they fulfilled blamelessly and with honor.

ANF 1, ed. A. Cleveland Coxe. Reprint, Peabody, MA: Hendrickson, 1994.

The Didache (Early Second Century)

The first three paragraphs of this selection from the *Didache* are concerned primarily with itinerant ministers and how they were to be treated. In a time when communication was slow, it would have been difficult to warn a congregation about a charlatan. Many Christian prophets and teachers would travel from one city to the next sharing their message. According to the *Didache,* such preachers were to be welcomed only if their teaching contributed to the righteous living of the church; otherwise they were to be turned away. Moreover, if a self-proclaimed prophet wanted to remain in a city for an extended period of time, or asked for money, he was to be rejected. Those who did come and reside in a location should be required to work, either practicing a trade or ministering to the people.

The *Didache* emphasized that the church was to be diligent in its selection of bishops and deacons. They were to be of outstanding Christian character because of the important job they had ministering to the community. Because of this position, they were to be treated with respect and honor. One finds here the same two officers as in Clement of Rome.

Chapter Eleven

Whoever comes and teaches you all these things that have been said before, receive him. But if the teacher himself should turn and teach another doctrine in opposition to this, do not listen to him. If he teaches in order to increase righteousness and the knowledge of the Lord, receive him as the Lord. But concerning the apostles and prophets, according to the decree of the Gospel, thus do. Let every apostle that comes to you be received as the Lord. But he should not stay longer than one day unless there is a need, when he can stay the next day. But if he remains three days, he is a false prophet. And when the apostle goes away, let him take nothing but bread until he lodges. If he asks for money, he is a false prophet. And every prophet that speaks in the Spirit you shall neither try nor judge; for every sin shall be forgiven, but this sin shall not be forgiven. But not every one that speaks in the Spirit is a prophet; but only if he holds the ways of the Lord. Therefore from their ways shall the false prophet and the prophet be known. And every prophet who orders a meal in the Spirit does not eat from it, except indeed he is a false prophet. Every prophet who teaches the truth, if he does not live what he teaches, is a false prophet. And every prophet, proved true, working unto the mystery of the Church in the world, yet not teaching others to do what he himself does, shall not be judged among you, for with God he has his judgment; for so did also the ancient prophets. But whoever says in the Spirit, Give me money, or something else, you shall not listen to him. But if he says to you to give for others' sake who are in need, let no one judge him.

Chapter Twelve

But let every one that comes in the name of the Lord be received, and afterward you shall prove and know him; for you shall have understanding right and left. If he who comes is a wayfarer, assist him as far as you are able; but he shall not remain with you, except for two or three days, if need be. But if he wishes to abide with you, being an artisan, let him work and eat; but if he has no trade, according to your understanding see to it that, as a Christian, he shall not live with you idle. But if he does not want to work he is a Christmonger. Watch that you keep aloof from such.

Chapter Thirteen

Every true prophet that wants to abide among you is worthy of his support. So also a true teacher is himself worthy, as the workman, of his support. Every first-fruit, therefore, of the products of wine-press and threshing-floor, of oxen and of sheep, you should take and give to the prophets, for they are your high priests. But if you do not have a prophet, give it to the poor. If you make a batch of dough, take the first-fruit and give according to the commandment. So also when you open a jar of wine or of oil, take the first-fruit and give it to the prophets; and of money and clothing and every possession, take the first-fruit, as it may seem good to you, and give according to the commandment.

Chapter Fifteen

Appoint for yourselves bishops and deacons worthy of the Lord, men who are meek, not lovers of money, truthful and proved. This is because they render to you the service of prophets and teachers. Do not despise them, for they are your honored ones, together with the prophets and teachers. Reprove one another, not in anger, but in peace, as you have it in the Gospel. Let no one speak to someone who acts amiss against someone else, nor let him hear anything from you until he repents. Pray and perform your alms and good deeds as you have been taught in the Gospel of our Lord.

ANF 7, ed. A. Cleveland Coxe. Reprint, Peabody, MA: Hendrickson, 1994.

Ignatius of Antioch (35–107)
Letter to the Trallians

In the letter below to the Christians in Tralles, in southern Asia Minor, Ignatius makes reference to the elders, deacons, and bishop. At this point, the bishop was still considered one of the elders. The bishop and the elders, who composed a body called the presbytery, had the responsibility of watching after the spiritual well-being of the community. Their authority was from God. Ignatius emphasized the importance of spiritual leaders in the community by stating that where there is no presbytery there is no church.

Concerning the deacons, he taught that their role was not merely to wait tables, serving food and drink, but rather to serve the church of God. Therefore, they were to live blameless lives. They were to be revered for the important role they played in church life, as ministers of the elements in the Eucharist.

An interesting statement concludes the selection. Ignatius told the Trallians that he did not issue orders like an apostle. One might consider that as a bishop he would have claimed apostolic authority, particularly after his prior comments on the authority of the bishop. Rather, he emphasized following one's own bishop, rather than following him.

Chapter Two

Be subject to the bishop as to the Lord, for "he watches for your souls, as one that shall give account to God." You also appear to me to live not after the manner of men, but according to Jesus Christ, who died for us, in order that, by believing in his death, you may by baptism be made partakers of his resurrection. It is therefore necessary, whatever you do, to do nothing without the bishop. And be subject also to the presbytery, as to the apostles of Jesus Christ, who is our hope, in whom, if we live, we shall be found in him. It behooves you also, in every way, to please the deacons, who are ministers of the mysteries of Christ Jesus; for they are not ministers of meat and drink, but servants of the church of God. They are bound, therefore, to avoid all grounds of accusation against them, as they would a burning fire. Let them, then, prove themselves to be such.

Chapter Three

Reverence them as Christ Jesus, of whose place they are the keepers, even as the bishop is the representative of the Father of all things, and the presbyters are the Sanhedrin of God, and assembly of the Apostles of Christ. Apart from these there is no elect church, no congregation of holy ones, no assembly of saints. I am persuaded that you also are of this opinion. For I have received the manifestation of your love, and still have it with me, in your bishop, whose very appearance is highly instructive, and his meekness of itself a power I imagine even the ungodly must reverence him. Loving you as I do, I avoid writing in any severer strain to you, that I may not seem harsh to any, or wanting in tenderness. I am indeed bound for the sake of Christ, but I am not yet worthy of Christ. But when I am perfected, perhaps I shall then become so. I do not issue orders like an apostle.

ANF 1, ed. A. Cleveland Coxe. Reprint, Peabody, MA: Hendrickson, 1994.

Polycarp of Smyrna (69–156)

Letter to the Philippians

Polycarp had hosted Ignatius of Antioch in Smyrna en route to Ignatius' execution in Rome. He was responsible for sending copies of Ignatius' seven letters to the Christians in Philippi. This passage is from the cover letter to that collection. Polycarp, whose subsequent martyrdom is described in detail in the *Martyrdom of Polycarp*, spoke of two offices in the church: presbyter and deacon. His emphases were the character of the deacon and the role of the presbyter. He provided a list of characteristics that leaders of the community were to possess, and a list of characteristics they should not possess. He also instructed the rest of the congregation to pursue the same positive characteristics as the leaders. The job of the presbyter was to reach out to the wandering member, to visit those who were sick, and to minister to the widow, the orphan, and the poor.

Chapter Five

Knowing, then, that "God is not mocked," we ought to walk worthy of his commandment and glory. In like manner should the deacons be blameless before the face of his righteousness, as being the servants of God and Christ, and not of men. They must not be slanderers, double-tongued, or lovers of money, but temperate in all things, compassionate, industrious, walking according to the truth of the Lord, who was the servant of all. If we please Him in this present world, we shall receive also the future world, according as he has promised to us that he will raise us again from the dead, and that if we live worthily of him, "we shall also reign together with him," provided only we believe. In like manner, let the young men also be blameless in all things, being especially careful to preserve purity, and reining themselves in, as with a bridle, from every kind of evil. For it is well that they should be cut off from the lusts that are in the world, since "every lust wars against the spirit"; and "neither fornicators, nor effeminate, nor abusers of themselves with mankind, shall inherit the kingdom of God," nor those who do things inconsistent and unbecoming. Therefore, we are to abstain from all these things, being subject to the presbyters and deacons, as unto God and Christ. The virgins also must walk in a blameless and pure conscience.

And let the presbyters be compassionate and merciful to all, bringing back those that wander, visiting all the sick, and not neglecting the widow, the orphan, or the poor, but always "providing for that which is becoming in the sight of God and humanity." Let them abstain from all wrath, respect of persons, and unjust judgment; keeping far off from all covetousness, not quickly crediting an evil report against any one, not severe in judgment, as knowing that we are all under a debt of sin. If then we entreat the Lord to forgive us, we ought also ourselves to forgive; for we are before the eyes of our Lord and God, and "we must all appear at the judgment seat of Christ, and must all give an account of himself." Let us then serve him in fear and with all reverence, even as he himself has commanded us, and as the apostles who preached the Gospel unto us, and the prophets who proclaimed beforehand the coming of the Lord have likewise taught us. Let us be zealous in the pursuit of that which is good, keeping ourselves from causes of offence, from false brethren, and from those who in hypocrisy bear the name of the Lord, and draw away vain men into error.

ANF 1, ed. A. Cleveland Coxe. Reprint, Peabody, MA: Hendrickson, 1994.

Cyprian of Carthage (200–258)
Letter 67

Cyprian's theme in this selection is the danger of divisive pastors who had split from the Christian community. He says that those who would follow the schismatic bishops would share in their sin of schism. To prevent the hijacking of the church by those who were unworthy, Cyprian instructed that leaders should be chosen publicly to afford everyone the opportunity to give testimony to the suitability of the candidate. Additionally, the ordination of a bishop would be valid only when bishops from neighboring churches were present. This would have ensured that the new bishop was in fellowship with the wider community of faith.

3. Do not let the people flatter themselves that they can be free from the contagion of sin, while communicating with a priest who is a sinner, and yielding their consent to the unjust and unlawful episcopacy of their overseer,

when the divine reproof by Hosea the prophet threatens, and says, "Their sacrifices shall be as the bread of mourning; all that eat thereof shall be polluted." The teaching is clear, showing that all are absolutely bound to the sin who have been contaminated by the sacrifice of a profane and unrighteous priest. Moreover, we find this clearly as well in Numbers, when Korah, and Dathan, and Abiram claimed for themselves the power of sacrificing in opposition to Aaron the priest. There also the Lord commanded by means of Moses that the people should be separated from them, lest, being associated with the wicked, themselves also should be bound closely in the same wickedness. "Separate yourselves," he said, "from the tents of these wicked and hardened men, and touch not those things which belong to them, lest you perish together in their sins." On which account a people obedient to the Lord's precepts, and fearing God, ought to separate themselves from a sinful prelate, and not to associate themselves with the sacrifices of a sacrilegious priest, especially since they themselves have the power either of choosing worthy priests, or of rejecting unworthy ones.

4. This very thing, too, we observe to come from divine authority, that the priest should be chosen in the presence of the people under the eyes of all, and should be approved worthy and suitable by public judgment and testimony. We find in the book of Numbers that the Lord commanded Moses, saying, "Take Aaron your brother, and Eleazar his son, and place them in the mount, in the presence of all the assembly, and strip Aaron of his garments, and put them upon Eleazar his son; and let Aaron die there, and be added to his people." God commands a priest to be appointed in the presence of all the assembly. He instructs and shows that the ordination of priests ought not to be solemnized except with the knowledge of the people standing near, that in the presence of the people either the crimes of the wicked may be disclosed, or the merits of the good may be declared, and the ordination, which shall have been examined by the suffrage and judgment of all, may be just and legitimate. This is subsequently observed, according to divine instruction, in the Acts of the Apostles, when Peter speaks to the people of ordaining an apostle in the place of Judas. "Peter," it says, "stood up in the midst of the disciples, and the multitude were in one place." Neither do we observe that this was regarded by the apostles only in the ordinations of bishops and priests, but also in those of deacons, of which matter itself also it is written in their Acts: "And they twelve called together the whole congregation of the disciples, and said to them. . . ." This was done diligently and carefully, with the calling together of the whole of the people, surely for the reason that no

unworthy person might creep into the ministry of the altar, or to the office of a priest. The fact that unworthy persons are sometimes ordained not according to the will of God but according to human presumption, and that those things which do not come of a legitimate and righteous ordination are displeasing to God, God himself makes abundantly clear by Hosea the prophet, when he says, "They have set up for themselves a king, but not by me."

5. For this reason you must diligently observe and keep the practice delivered from divine tradition and apostolic observance, which is also maintained among us, and throughout almost all the provinces. For the proper celebration of ordinations all the neighboring bishops of the same province should assemble with that people for which a prelate is ordained. The bishop should be chosen in the presence of the people, who have most fully known the life of each one, and have looked into the doings of each one as respects his habitual conduct.

ANF 5, ed. A. Cleveland Coxe. Reprint, Peabody, MA: Hendrickson, 1994.

Apostolic Constitutions (Fourth Century)

Three primary offices are described in the *Apostolic Constitutions*: bishop, presbyter, and deacon. There are additional instructions for deaconesses, subdeacons, readers, and singers. The roles of the bishop and the presbyter were the same with the exception of the bishop's authority to rule. This would be compatible with the notion of the bishop's being one of the elders (*primus inter pares*). Their responsibilities included teaching the community and administering the sacraments of baptism and the Eucharist. The deacons and deaconesses were instructed to visit those who were sick and to assist the bishop. Subdeacons were aides to the deacons and deaconesses, and the readers and singers participated in public worship through the reading of the Scriptures and singing, respectively.

Central to the instructions given here is the importance of a blameless character, including frugality and humility. The church leaders were to be examples to the other members and thus should practice right living. Besides exemplary living, bishops should be at least fifty years old. The author indicates that this was to prevent a bishop from falling victim to the temptations of youth. There were instances, such as a small town or where there is a paucity of candidates, where a younger man may have been chosen, but these were exceptions.

Ordination of bishops should have taken place in the presence of at least two other bishops, and preferably three, in order to have had adequate testimony to the candidate's character. Elders and deacons were to be ordained by the bishop along with the other clergy from the church.

An interesting set of requirements revolves around the marriage of the clergy. Bishops, presbyters, and deacons were permitted to marry, but only once. If they were not married when they took office, the *Constitutions* did not permit them to marry subsequently. Even after the death of a spouse, they were not permitted to remarry. Deaconesses must either have never been married or have been widowed. The other officers were allowed to marry at any time, but only once.

Book Two

1. Concerning bishops, we have heard from our Lord that a pastor who is to be ordained a bishop for the churches in every parish must be blameless, unreprovable, and free from all kinds of wickedness common among men. He should not be under fifty years of age, for such a one is in good part past youthful disorders and the slanders of the heathen. Likewise, he is beyond the reproaches which are sometimes cast upon many persons by some false brethren who do not consider the word of God in the Gospel: "Whosoever speaks an idle word shall give an account to the Lord for it in the day of judgment." And again: "By your own words you will be justified, and by your words you will be condemned." Let him, if it is possible, be well educated; but if he be unlettered, let him at any rate be skillful in the word, and of competent age. If in a small parish one advanced in years is not available, let a younger person who has a good report among his neighbors and is esteemed by them worthy of the office of a bishop be ordained in peace. He should have carried himself from his youth with meekness and regularity, like a much older person. He should be ordained only after examination and a general good report. Remember that Solomon was king of Israel at twelve years of age, and Josiah at eight years of age reigned righteously. Moreover, Joash governed the people at seven years of age. Therefore, although the person be young, let him be meek, gentle, and quiet. For the Lord God says by Isaiah: "Upon whom will I look, but upon him who is humble and quiet, and always trembles at my words?" In like manner it is in the Gospel also: "Blessed are

the meek, for they shall inherit the earth." Let him also be merciful; for again it is said: "Blessed are the merciful, for they shall obtain mercy." Let him also be a peacemaker; for again it is said: "Blessed are the peacemakers, for they shall be called sons of God." Let him also be one of a good conscience, purified from all evil, wickedness, and unrighteousness; for it is said again: "Blessed are the pure in heart, for they shall see God."

2. Let him therefore be sober, prudent, decent, firm, stable, and not given to wine. He should not be a striker, but gentle. Nor should he be a brawler or covetous. He should "not be a novice, lest, being puffed up with pride, he falls into condemnation, and the snare of the devil: for every one that exalts himself shall be abased." A bishop ought to be one who has been the "husband of one wife." His wife should have had no other husband. He should also "rule well his own house." In this manner let examination be made when he is to receive ordination, and to be placed in his bishopric, whether he is grave, faithful, and decent. Whether he has a grave and faithful wife, or has formerly had such a one. Whether he has educated his children piously, and has "brought them up in the nurture and admonition of the Lord." Whether his domestics do fear and reverence him, and are all obedient to him. If those who are immediately around him for worldly concerns are seditious and disobedient, how will others not of his family, when they are under his management, become obedient to him? . . .

5. Let a bishop be frugal, and contented with moderate amounts of food and drink, in order that he may always be of a sober disposition, and disposed to instruct and admonish the ignorant. Let him not be costly in his diet, pampered, given to pleasure, or fond of delicacies. Let him he patient and gentle in his admonitions, well instructed himself, meditating in and diligently studying the Lord's books, reading them frequently, so that he may be able carefully to interpret the Scriptures, expounding the Gospel in correspondence with the prophets and with the law; and let the expositions from the law and the prophets correspond to the Gospel. . . .

6. Do not let a bishop be given to filthy lucre, especially before the Gentiles. He should suffer injuries rather than offer them. He should not be covetous, nor rapacious; no purloiner; no admirer of the rich, nor hater of the poor; no evil-speaker, nor false witness; not given to anger; no brawler; not entangled with the affairs of this life; not a surety for any one, nor an accuser in suits about money; not ambitious; not double-minded, nor double-tongued; not ready to hearken to calumny or evil-speaking; not a dissembler; not addicted to the heathen festivals; not given to vain deceits; not eager after

worldly things, nor a lover of money. All these things are opposed to God, and pleasing to demons. Let the bishop earnestly give all these precepts in charge to the laity also, persuading them to imitate his conduct. For God says, "Make the children of Israel pious." Let him be prudent, humble, apt to admonish with the instructions of the Lord, well-disposed, one who has renounced all the wicked projects of this world, and all heathenish desires. Let him be orderly, sharp in observing the wicked, and taking heed of them, but yet a friend to all. Let him be just and discerning. Let the bishop possess in himself whatever qualities are commendable among humanity. This is because if the pastor is blameless as to any wickedness, he will compel his own disciples, and by his very manner of life persuade them to become worthy imitators of his own actions. As the prophet somewhere says, "And it will be, as is the priest, so is the people." Our Lord and Teacher Jesus Christ, the Son of God, began first to do, and then to teach, as Luke somewhere says, "which Jesus began to do and to teach." Therefore he says, "Whosoever shall do and teach, he shall be called great in the kingdom of God." For you bishops are to be guides and watchmen to the people, as you yourselves have Christ for your guide and watchman. Do you therefore become good guides and watchmen to the people of God. . . .

31. Let the deacon not do anything at all without his bishop, nor give anything without his consent. For if he gives to any one as to a person in distress without the bishop's knowledge, he gives it so that it must tend to the reproach of the bishop, and he accuses him as careless of the distressed. But he that casts reproach on his bishop, either by word or deed, opposes God, not heeding what he says: "You shall not speak evil of the gods." For he did not make that law concerning deities of wood and of stone, which are abominable, because they are falsely called gods, but concerning the priests and the judges, to whom he also said, "You are gods, and children of the Most High."

Book Three

19. Let the deacons be in all things unspotted, as the bishop himself is to be, only more active; in number according to the largeness of the church, in order that they may minister to the infirm as workmen that are not ashamed. And let the deaconess be diligent in taking care of the women; but both of them ready to carry messages, to travel about, to minister, and to serve, as spoke Isaiah concerning the Lord: "To justify the righteous, who serves many faithfully." Let every one therefore know his proper

place, and discharge it diligently with one consent, with one mind, as knowing the reward of their ministration; but let them not be ashamed to minister to those that are in want, as even our "Lord Jesus Christ came not to be ministered unto, but to minister and to give his life a ransom for many." So therefore ought they also to do, and not to avoid it, if they should be obliged to lay down their life for a brother or sister in Christ. For the Lord and our Savior Jesus Christ did not have a problem with "laying down his life for his friends," as he himself says. If, therefore, the Lord of heaven and earth underwent all his sufferings for us, how then do you make a difficulty to minister to such as are in want, who ought to imitate him who underwent servitude, and want, and stripes, and the cross for us? We ought therefore also to serve the brethren, in imitation of Christ. For he says, "He that will be great among you, let him be your minister; and he that will be first among you, let him be your servant." He did in reality, and not in word only, fulfill the prediction of "serving many faithfully." For "when he had taken a towel, he girded himself. Afterward he put water into a basin; and as we were sitting at the meal he came and washed the feet of us all, and wiped them with the towel." By doing this he demonstrated to us his kindness and brotherly affection, so that we also might do the same to one another. If, therefore, our Lord and Master so humbled himself, how can you, the laborers of the truth and administrators of piety, be ashamed to do the same to such of the brethren as are weak and infirm? Minister therefore with a kind mind, not murmuring nor mutinying; for you do not do it on the account of man, but on the account of God, and shall receive from him the reward of your ministry in the day of your visitation. It is your duty who are deacons to visit all those who stand in need of visitation. And tell your bishop of all those that are in affliction; for you ought to be like his soul and senses, active and attentive in all things to him as father and master.

20. We command that a bishop be ordained by three bishops, or at least by two. It is not lawful that he be set over you by one, for the testimony of two or three witnesses is more firm and secure. But a presbyter and a deacon are to be ordained by one bishop and the rest of the clergy. Neither a presbyter or a deacon ordain from the laity into the clergy. The presbyter is only to teach, to offer, to baptize, to bless the people. The deacon is to minister to the bishop, and to the presbyters, that is, to do the office of a ministering deacon, but not to meddle with the other offices.

Book Six

17. We have already said that a bishop, a presbyter, and a deacon, when they are constituted, must be but once married, whether their wives be alive or whether they be dead. It is not lawful for them, if they are unmarried when they are ordained, to be married afterwards. If they are married when they are ordained, they are not to marry a second time, but to be content with the wife that they had when they came to ordination. We also instruct that the ministers, singers, readers, and porters shall be married only once. But if they entered into the clergy before they were married, we permit them to marry, if they have an inclination to do so, lest they sin and incur punishment. We do not permit any one of the clergy to take as his wife a courtesan, a servant, a widow, or one that is divorced, as also the law says. Let the deaconess be a pure virgin, or at the least a widow who has been married only once. She should be faithful and well esteemed.

Book Eight

16. Concerning the ordination of presbyters, I who am loved by the Lord make this constitution for you the bishops: When you ordain a presbyter, O bishop, lay your hand upon his head, in the presence of the presbyters and deacons, and pray, saying, "O Lord Almighty, our God, who has created all things by Christ, and likewise does take care of the whole world by him; for he who had power to make different creatures, has also power to take care of them, according to their different natures; on which account, O God, you take care of immortal beings by bare preservation, but of those that are mortal by succession—of the soul by the provision of laws, of the body by the supply of its wants. Therefore look down now upon your holy church and increase it. Multiply those that preside in it. Grant them power that they may labor both in word and work for the edification of your people. Look down now upon this your servant, who is put into the presbytery by the vote and determination of the whole clergy. Replenish him with the Spirit of grace and counsel to assist and govern your people with a pure heart in the same manner as you looked down upon your chosen people, and commanded Moses to choose elders whom you filled with your Spirit. O Lord, grant this and preserve in us the Spirit of your grace, that this person, being filled with the gifts of healing and the word of teaching, may in

meekness instruct your people, and sincerely serve you with a pure mind and a willing soul, and may fully discharge the holy ministrations for your people, through your Christ, with whom glory, honor, and worship be to you, and to the Holy Spirit, for ever. Amen.

17. Concerning the ordination of deacons, I Philip make this constitution: You shall ordain a deacon, O bishop, by laying your hands upon him in the presence of the whole presbytery, and of the deacons, and shall pray, and say:

18. "O God Almighty, the true and faithful God, who is rich unto all that call upon you in truth, who is fearful in counsels, and wise in understanding, who is powerful and great, hear our prayer, O Lord, and let your ears receive our supplication. 'Cause the light of your countenance to shine upon this your servant,' who is to be ordained for you to the office of a deacon. Replenish him with your Holy Spirit and with power, as you replenished Stephen, who was your martyr and follower of the sufferings of your Christ. Render him worthy to discharge acceptably the ministration of a deacon, steadily, blamelessly, and without reproof, that thereby he may attain a higher degree, through the mediation of your only begotten Son, with whom glory, honor, and worship be to you and the Holy Spirit for ever. Amen."

19. Concerning a deaconess, I Bartholomew make this constitution: O bishop, you shall lay your hands upon her in the presence of the presbytery, and of the deacons and deaconesses, and shall say:

20. "O Eternal God, the Father of our Lord Jesus Christ, the Creator of man and of woman, who replenished with the Spirit Miriam, Deborah, Anna, and Huldah; who did not disdain that your only begotten Son should be born of a woman; who also in the tabernacle of the testimony, and in the temple, ordained women to be keepers of your holy gates, look down now upon this your servant, who is to be ordained to the office of a deaconess, and grant her your Holy Spirit, and 'cleanse her from all filthiness of flesh and spirit,' that she may worthily discharge the work which is committed to her to your glory, and the praise of your Christ, with whom glory and adoration be to you and the Holy Spirit for ever. Amen."

21. Concerning the sub-deacons, I Thomas make this constitution for you the bishops: When you ordain a sub-deacon, O bishop, you shall lay your hands upon him, and say: "O Lord God, the Creator of heaven and earth, and of all things that are therein; who also in the tabernacle of the testimony appointed overseers and keepers of your holy vessels; look down now upon this your servant, appointed a sub-deacon. Grant him the Holy Spirit, that he may worthily handle the vessels of your ministry, and do your will always,

through your Christ, with whom glory, honor, and worship be to you and to the Holy Spirit for ever. Amen."

22. Concerning readers, I Matthew, also called Levi, who was once a tax-gatherer, make a constitution: Ordain a reader by laying your hands upon him, and pray unto God, and say: "O Eternal God, who is plenteous in mercy and compassions, who has made clear the constitution of the world by your operations therein, and keep the number of your elect, look down now upon your servant, who is to be entrusted to read your Holy Scriptures to your people, and give him your Holy Spirit, the prophetic Spirit. You who instructed Ezra your servant to read your laws to the people, now also at our prayers instruct your servant, and grant that he may without blame perfect the work committed to him, and thereby be declared worthy of a higher degree, through Christ, with whom glory and worship be to you and to the Holy Spirit for ever. Amen." . . .

27. And I Simon the Canaanite make a constitution to determine by how many a bishop ought to be elected. Let a bishop be ordained by three or two bishops; but if any one be ordained by one bishop, let him be deprived, both himself and he that ordained him. But if there be a necessity that he have only one to ordain him, because more bishops cannot come together, as in time of persecution, or for such like causes, let him bring the suffrage of permission from more bishops.

28. Concerning the canons I the same make a constitution. A bishop blesses, but does not receive the blessing. He lays on hands, ordains, offers, receives the blessing from bishops, but by no means from presbyters. A bishop deprives any clergyman who deserves deprivation, excepting a bishop; for of himself he does not have the power to do that. A presbyter blesses, but does not receive the blessing; yet he does receive the blessing from the bishop or a fellow-presbyter. In like manner he gives it to a fellow-presbyter. He lays on hands, but does not ordain; he does not deprive, yet he does separate those that are under him, if they be liable to such a punishment. A deacon does not bless, does not give the blessing, but receives it from the bishop and presbyter: he does not baptize, he does not offer; but when a bishop or presbyter has offered, he distributes to the people, not as a priest, but as one that ministers to the priests. It is not lawful for any one of the other clergy to do the work of a deacon. A deaconess does not bless, nor perform anything belonging to the office of presbyters or deacons, but only is to keep the doors and to minister to the presbyters in the baptizing of women, on account of decency. A deacon separates a sub-deacon, a reader, a singer, and a deaconess, if

there is any reason for doing so in the absence of a presbyter. It is not lawful for a sub-deacon to separate either one of the clergy or laity; nor for a reader, nor for a singer, nor for a deaconess, for they are the ministers to the deacons.

ANF 7, ed. A. Cleveland Coxe. Reprint, Peabody, MA: Hendrickson, 1994.

Jerome (342–420)
Letter 146

Here Jerome is concerned with a particular Roman practice of ordaining only those who had been recommended by a deacon to be an elder. This was obviously not standard practice, as Jerome points out. The usual manner would be to choose a deacon to ordain as an elder. Jerome not only provides a picture of the clergy in his own day but also rehearses the standard practice prior to his time. He states that the New Testament refers to bishop and presbyter as the same office. Eventually, in order to prevent schism, one of the elders was chosen by them to serve as the bishop, in the manner that an army selected one of its number to be the general. The only function the bishop had that the other presbyters did not have was that of ordination. In their New Testament usage, Jerome says that the term "elder" referred to age and the term "bishop" referred to rank in the church. The office of bishop included the office of presbyter.

1. We read in Isaiah the words "the fool will speak folly," and I am told that some one has been mad enough to put deacons before presbyters, that is, before bishops. For when the apostle clearly teaches that presbyters are the same as bishops, must not a mere server of tables and of widows be insane to set himself up arrogantly over men through whose prayers the body and blood of Christ are produced? Do you ask for proof of what I say? Listen to this passage: "Paul and Timothy, the servants of Jesus Christ, to all the saints in Christ Jesus which are at Philippi with the bishops and deacons." Do you wish for another instance? In the Acts of the Apostles Paul thus speaks to the priests of a single church: "Take heed unto yourselves and to all the flock, in which the Holy Spirit has made you bishops, to feed the church of God which he purchased with his own blood." And lest any should in a spirit of contention argue that there must then have been more bishops than one in a sin-

gle church, there is the following passage which clearly proves a bishop and a presbyter to be the same. Writing to Titus, the apostle says, "For this cause left I you in Crete, that you should set in order the things that are wanting, and ordain presbyters in every city, as I had appointed you: if any be blameless, the husband of one wife, having faithful children not accused of riot or unruly. For a bishop must be blameless as the steward of God." And to Timothy he says, "Do not neglect the gift that is in you, which was given you by prophecy, with the laying on of the hands of the presbytery." Peter also says in his first epistle, "I who am your fellow-presbyter and a witness of the sufferings of Christ and also a partaker of the glory that shall be revealed exhort the presbyters which are among you to feed the flock of Christ, taking the oversight of the flock not by constraint but willingly, according unto God." In the Greek the meaning is still plainer, for the word used is episcopate, that is to say, overseeing. This is the origin of the name overseer or bishop. But perhaps the testimony of these great men seems to you insufficient. If so, then listen to the blast of the gospel trumpet, that son of thunder, the disciple whom Jesus loved and who reclining on the Savior's breast drank in the waters of sound doctrine. One of his letters begins this way: "The presbyter to the elect lady and her children whom I love in the truth." Another begins this way: "The presbyter to the well-beloved Gaius whom I love in the truth." When subsequently one presbyter was chosen to preside over the rest, this was done to remedy schism and to prevent each individual from rending the church of Christ by drawing it to himself. For even at Alexandria from the time of Mark the Evangelist until the episcopates of Heraclas and Dionysius the presbyters always named as bishop one of their own number chosen by themselves and set in a more exalted position, just as an army elects a general, or as deacons appoint one of themselves whom they know to be diligent and call him archdeacon. For what function other than ordination, belongs to a bishop that does not also belong to a presbyter? It is not the case that there is one church at Rome and another in all the world beside. Gaul and Britain, Africa and Persia, India and the East worship one Christ and observe one rule of truth. If you ask for authority, the world outweighs its capital. Wherever there is a bishop, whether it be at Rome or at Engubium, whether it be at Constantinople or at Rhegium, whether it be at Alexandria or at Zoan, his dignity is one and his priesthood is one. Neither the command of wealth nor the lowliness of poverty makes him more a bishop or less a bishop. All alike are successors of the apostles.

2. But you will say, how then does it come that at Rome a presbyter is only ordained on the recommendation of a deacon? To which I reply as follows: why do you bring forward a custom which exists in one city only? Why do you oppose to the laws of the Church a paltry exception which has given rise to arrogance and pride? The more rare something is the more it is sought after. In India pennyroyal is more costly than pepper. Their paucity makes deacons persons of consequence while presbyters are less thought of owing to their great numbers. But even in the church of Rome the deacons stand while the presbyters seat themselves, although bad habits have by degrees so far crept in that I have seen a deacon, in the absence of the bishop, seat himself among the presbyters and at social gatherings give his blessing to them. Those who act this way must learn that they are wrong and must give heed to the apostles' words: "It is not fitting that we should leave the word of God and serve tables." They must consider the reasons which led to the appointment of deacons at the beginning. They must read the Acts of the Apostles and bear in mind their true position. Of the names presbyter and bishop the first denotes age, the second rank. In writing both to Titus and to Timothy the apostle speaks of the ordination of bishops and of deacons, but says not a word of the ordination of presbyters. The fact is that the word bishops includes presbyters also. Again when a man is promoted it is from a lower place to a higher. Either then a presbyter should be ordained a deacon, from the lesser office, that is, to the more important, to prove that a presbyter is inferior to a deacon. If on the other hand it is the deacon that is ordained presbyter, this latter should recognize that although he may be less highly paid than a deacon, he is superior to him in virtue of his priesthood. In fact as if to tell us that the traditions handed down by the apostles were taken by them from the Old Testament, bishops, presbyters and deacons occupy in the church the same positions as those which were occupied by Aaron, his sons, and the Levites in the temple.

NPNF 2.6, ed. W. Sanday. Reprint, Peabody, MA: Hendrickson, 1994.

Jerome (342–420)

Against Jovinianus

In this selection, Jerome emphasizes the importance of the character of the church leaders. Good character was necessary, Jerome argues, because the value of the ministry was not in the office one held, but the virtue one possessed. The good works of a minister were more important than the title that one had been given.

35. The bishop, then, must be "without reproach," so that he is the slave of no vice. He must be "the husband of one wife," that is, in the past not in the present. He must be "sober," or better, as it is in the Greek, "vigilant." He must be "chaste," for that is the meaning of the Greek term; "distinguished," both by chastity and conduct; "hospitable," so that he imitates Abraham, and with strangers, or rather in strangers, entertains Christ; "apt to teach," for it profits nothing to enjoy the consciousness of virtue, unless a man be able to instruct the people entrusted to him, so that he can exhort in doctrine, and refute the gainsayers; "not a drunkard," for he who is constantly in the Holy of Holies and offers sacrifices, will not drink wine and strong drink, since wine is a luxury. If a bishop drink at all, let it be in such a way that no one will know whether he has drunk or not. He must be "no striker," that is, a striker of men's consciences, for the Apostle is not pointing out what a boxer, but a pontiff ought not to do. He directly teaches what he ought to do: "gentle, not contentious, no lover of money, one that rules well his own house, having his children in subjection with all chastity." See what chastity is required in a bishop! If his child be unchaste, he himself cannot be a bishop, and he offends God in the same way as did Eli the priest, who had indeed rebuked his sons, but because he had not put away the offenders, fell backwards and died before the lamp of God went out. "Women in like manner must be chaste," and so on. In every grade, and in both sexes, chastity has the chief place. You see then that the blessedness of a bishop, priest, or deacon, does not lie in the fact that they are bishops, priests, or deacons, but in their having the virtues which their names and offices imply. Otherwise, if a deacon is holier than his bishop, his lower grade will not give him a worse standing with Christ. If it were so, Stephen the deacon, the first to wear the martyr's crown, would be less in the kingdom of heaven than many bishops, and than Timothy and Titus, whom I venture to make neither inferior nor yet superior to him. Just as in the legions of the army there are generals, tribunes, centurions, javelin-men, and light-armed troops, common soldiers, and companies, but once the battle begins, all distinctions of rank are dropped, and the one thing looked for is valor. So too in this camp and in this battle, in which we contend against devils, not simply titles, but works are needed.

Under the true commander, Christ, not the man who has the highest title has the greatest fame, but he who is the bravest warrior.

NPNF 2.6, ed. W. Sanday. Reprint, Peabody, MA: Hendrickson, 1994.

John Chrysostom of Constantinople (347–407)
On the Priesthood

John exposes two inappropriate reasons for entering the ministry: selfish ambition and coercion. In the first instance, even if one were to be asked by countless people to serve in a particular position, he should first ensure that he did not do so out of misguided desires. If one obtained a position through his ambition, he would inevitably bring shame to the office of elder through either his laziness, his sin, or his inexperience. No one would try to build a building or cure someone who was ill without the appropriate training, he argues. If coerced into the position, the elder would share in the sins of those who forced him to do it.

There is also a long explanation of why the pastor should be skilled in the exposition of Scripture. It was not enough, John says, for the pastor to have a blameless character if he were to be unable to defend the Christian faith against false teachers. Moreover, it was the responsibility of the minister to teach the other members of the church how to articulate the true gospel and to defend their beliefs.

Book Four

1. I beseech and implore you, do not be so downcast. For while there is safety for us who are weak, namely, in not undertaking this office at all, there is safety for you too who are strong. This consists in making your hopes of salvation depend, next to the grace of God, on avoiding every act unworthy of this gift, and of God who gave it. For they certainly would be deserving of the greatest punishment who, after obtaining this dignity through their own ambition, should then either on account of sloth, or wickedness, or even inexperience, abuse the office. Not that we are to gather from this that there is pardon in store for those who have not been thus ambitious. Yea, even they too are deprived of all excuse. For in my judgment, if ten thousand were to entreat and urge, a man should pay them no attention, but should first of all

search his own heart, and examine the whole matter carefully before yielding to their importunities. Now no one would venture to undertake the building of a house if he were not an architect, nor will any one attempt the cure of sick bodies who is not a skilled physician. Even though many urge him, he will beg off, and will not be ashamed to own his ignorance. Shall the one who is going to have the care of so many souls entrusted to him, not examine himself beforehand? Will he accept this ministry even if he is the most inexperienced of men simply because this one commands him, or that one constrains him, or for fear of offending a third? And if so, how will he escape casting himself together with them into manifest misery. Had he continued as he was, it were possible for him to be saved, but now he involves others in his own destruction. For from where can he hope for salvation? From where does he obtain pardon? Who will then successfully intercede for us? They who are now perhaps urging us and forcibly dragging us on? But who will save these same at such a moment? For even they too will stand in need in their turn of intercession, that they may escape the fire. Now, that I say not these things to frighten you, but as representing the matter as in truth it is, hear what the holy Apostle Paul says to Timothy his disciple, his own and beloved son: "Lay hands suddenly on no man, neither be partaker of other men's sins." Do you not see from what great blame and vengeance, we, so far as in us lies, have delivered those who were ready to put us forward for this office. . . .

8. Hear also what he says in his charge to his disciple: "Give heed to reading, to exhortation, to teaching." He goes on to show the usefulness of this by adding, "For in doing this you will save both yourself and those that hear you." Again he says, "The Lord's servant must not strive, but be gentle towards all, apt to teach, forbearing"; and he proceeds to say, "But abide in the things which you have learned, and have been assured of, knowing of whom you have learned them, and that from a babe you have known the sacred writings which are able to make you wise unto salvation." Again he says, "Every Scripture is inspired of God, and also profitable for teaching, for reproof, for correction, for instruction which is in righteousness, that the man of God may be complete." Hear what he adds further in his directions to Titus about the appointment of bishops. "The bishop," he says, "must be holding to the faithful word which is according to the teaching, that he may be able to convict the gainsayers." But how shall any one who is unskillful as these men pretend be able to convict the gainsayers and stop their mouths? What need is there to give attention to reading and to the Holy Scriptures, if such a state of unskillfulness is to be welcome among us? Such arguments are mere

makeshifts and pretexts, the marks of idleness and sloth. But someone will say, "It is to the priests that these charges are given." Certainly this is so, for they are the subjects of our discourse. But that the apostle gives the same charge to the laity, hear what he says in another epistle to other than the priesthood: "Let the word of Christ dwell in you richly in all wisdom," and again, "Let your speech be always with grace seasoned with salt, that you may know how you ought to answer each one." In addition, there is a general charge to all that they "be ready to" render an account of their faith, and to the Thessalonians, he gives the following command: "Build each other up, even as also you do." But when he speaks of priests he says, "Let the elders that rule well be counted worthy of double honor, especially those who labor in the word, and in teaching." This is the perfection of teaching when the teachers both by what they do, and by what they say as well, bring their disciples to that blessed state of life which Christ appointed for them. Example alone is not enough to instruct others. Nor do I say this of myself; it is our Savior's own word: "For whoever shall do and teach them, he shall be called great." Now if doing were the same as teaching, the second word here would be superfluous; and it had been enough to have said "whoever shall do" simply. But now by distinguishing the two, he shows that practice is one thing, and doctrine another, and that each needs the help of the other in order to complete edification. Hear too what the chosen vessel of Christ says to the Ephesian elders: "Therefore watch yourself, remembering that for the space of three years, I ceased not to admonish every one, night and day, with tears." But what need was there for his tears or for admonition by word of mouth, while his life as an apostle was so illustrious? His holy life might be a great inducement to men to keep the commandments, yet I dare not say that it alone could accomplish everything.

9. But when a dispute arises concerning matters of doctrine, and all take their weapons from the same Scriptures, of what weight will any one's life be able to prove? What then will be the good of his many austerities, when after such painful exercises anyone should fall into heresy and be cut off from the body of the church as a result of the priest's great unskillfulness in argument? I have myself seen many suffer this misfortune. Of what profit then will his patience be to him? No more than there will be in a sound faith if the life is corrupt. Therefore, for this reason more than for all others it concerns him whose office it is to teach others to be experienced in disputations of this kind. For though he himself stands safely and is unhurt by the gainsayers, the simple multitude under his direction, when they see their leader defeated and

without any answer for the gainsayers, will be apt to lay the blame of his dis-comfiture not on his own weakness but on the doctrines themselves, as though they were faulty. Consequently, great numbers are brought to ex-treme ruin through the inexperience of one. Though they do not entirely go over to the adversary, they are forced to doubt about matters in which for-merly they firmly believed. Those whom they used to approach with unswerving confidence, now they are unable to hold to any longer steadfastly, but in consequence of their leader's defeat, so great a storm settles down upon their souls, that the mischief ends in their shipwreck altogether. But how dire is the destruction, and how terrible the fire which such a leader brings upon his own wretched head for every soul which is thus lost, you will not need to learn from me, as you know all this perfectly. Is this then pride, is this vain-glory in me, to be unwilling to be the cause of the destruction of so many souls, and of procuring for myself greater punishment in the world to come, than that which now awaits me there? Who would say so? Surely no one, un-less he should wish to find fault where there is none, and to moralize over other men's calamities.

NPNF 1.9, ed. Philip Schaff. Reprint, Peabody, MA: Hendrickson, 1994.

John Chrysostom of Constantinople (347–407)
Homily Ten on 1 Timothy

Chrysostom sought here to concentrate his attention on the character of church officers. The first selection relates to the bishop. John explains that the bishop was to have impeccable character because the protection of the church rested on his shoulders. He echoes the sentiments of previous writ-ers in his assessment of the importance of the pastors. It was not their po-litical influence he sought but the influence of their lives, which could be used either for the good of the community or its demise.

Proceeding to discourse of the Episcopal office, he sets out with showing what sort of a person a Bishop ought to be. And here he does not do it as in the course of his exhortation to Timothy, but addresses all, and instructs oth-ers through him. And what does he say? "If a man desire the office of a Bishop," I do not blame him, for it is a work of protection. If any one has this desire, so that he does not covet the dominion and authority, but wishes to protect the Church, I blame him not. "For he desires a good work." Even Moses desired the office, though not the power, and his desire exposed him to that taunt, "Who made you a ruler and a judge over us?" If any one, then, desire it in this way, let him desire it. For the Episcopate is so called from having the oversight of all.

"A Bishop then," he says, "must be blameless, the husband of one wife." He does not lay this down as a rule, as if he must not be without one, but as prohibiting his having more than one. For even the Jews were allowed to contract second marriages, and even to have two wives at one time. For "marriage is honorable." Some, however say that this is said that he should be the husband of one wife. "Blameless." Every virtue is implied in this word; so that if any one be conscious to himself of any sins, he ought not to desire an office for which his own actions have disqualified him. For such a one ought to be ruled, and not to rule others. For he who bears rule should be brighter than any luminary; his life should be unspotted, so that all should look up to him, and make his life the model of their own. But in employing this exhortation, he had no common object in view. For he too was about to appoint Bishops (which also he exhorts Titus to do in his Letter to him), and as it was probable that many would desire that office, therefore he urges these admonitions. "Vigilant," he says, that is, circumspect, having a thousand eyes about him, quick sighted, not having the eyes of his mind dimmed. For many things occur which permit not a man to see clearly, to see things as they are. For care and troubles, and a load of business on all sides press upon him. He must therefore be vigilant, not only over his own concerns, but over those of others. He must be well awake, he must be fervent in spirit, and, as it were, breathe fire; he must labor and attend upon his duty by day and by night, even more than a general upon his army; he must be careful and concerned for all. "Sober, of good behavior, given to hospitality." Because these qualities are possessed by most of those who are under their rule (for in these respects they ought to be equal to those who rule over them), he, to show what is peculiar to the Bishops, adds, "apt to teach." For this is not required of him that is ruled, but is most essential to him who has this rule committed to him.

"Not given to wine." Here he does not so much mean intemperate, as insolent and impudent. "No striker." This too does not mean a striker with the hands. What means then "no striker"? Because there are some who unseasonably smite the consciences of their brethren, it seems to be said with reference to them. "Not greedy of filthy lucre, but patient. Not a brawler, not covetous, one that rules his own house well, having his children in subjection with all gravity." If then "he who is married cares for the things of the world," and a Bishop ought not to care for the things of the world, why does he say the husband of one wife? Some indeed think that he says this with reference to one who remains free from a wife. But if otherwise, he that has a wife may be as though he had none. For that liberty was then properly granted, as suited to the nature of the circumstances then existing. And it is very possible, if a man will, so to regulate his conduct. For as riches make it difficult to enter into the kingdom of Heaven, yet rich men have often entered in, so it is with marriage. But why does he say, speaking of a Bishop, that he should be "not given to wine, hospitable," when he should name greater things? Why did he not say that he should be an Angel, not subject to human passions? Where are those great qualities of which Christ speaks, which even those under their rule ought to possess? To be crucified to the world, to be always ready to lay down their lives, as Christ said. "The good Shepherd gives his life for the sheep." Again he says, "He that does not take up his cross and follow after me, is not worthy of me." But "not given to wine," he says; a good prospect indeed, if such are the things of which a Bishop is to be admonished! Why has he not said that he ought to be already raised above the world? But do you demand less of the Bishop, than even of those in the world? For to these he said, "Mortify your members which are upon the earth," and "He that is dead, is freed from sin." "They that are Christ's have crucified the flesh," and Christ again says, "Whosoever forsakes not all that he has, he is not worthy of me." Why are these things not required by Paul? Plainly because few could be found of such a character, and there was need of many Bishops, that one might preside in every city.

But because the churches were to be exposed to attacks, he does not require that superior and highly exalted virtue, but a moderate degree of it. For to be sober, of good behavior, and temperate were qualities common to many. "Having his children in subjection with all gravity." This is necessary, that an example might be exhibited in his own house. For who would believe that he who had not his own son in subjection, would keep a stranger under command? "One that rules his own house well." Even those who are without say this, that he who is a good manager of a house will be a good statesman. For the church is, as it were, a small household, and as in a house there are children and wife and domestics, and the man has rule over them all. Likewise in the church there are women, children, and servants. If he that presides in the church has partners in his power, so has the man a partner, that is, his wife. Ought the church to provide for her widows and virgins just as in a family there are servants and daughters to be provided for. In fact, it is easier to rule the house. Therefore he asks, "If a man does not know how to rule his own house, how shall he take care of the church of God?"

Verse 6. "Not a novice." He does not say, not a young man, but not a new convert. For he had said, "I have planted, Apollos watered, but God gave the increase." Wishing them to point out such a one, he used this word. For, otherwise, what hindered him from saying, "Not a young man"? For if youth only was an objection, why did he himself appoint Timothy, who is a young man, a fact demonstrated by Paul's statement, "Let no man despise your youth." It was because he was aware of his great virtue, and his great strictness of life. Knowing which he writes, "From a child you have learned the holy Scriptures." And that he practiced intense fasting is proved by the words, "Use a little wine for your frequent infirmities." This he wrote to him among other things as if he had not known of such good works of his, he would not have written, nor given any such charge to his disciple. But as there were many then who came over from the heathen, and were baptized, he says, "Do not immediately advance to a station of dignity a novice, that is, one of these new converts." For, if before he had well been a disciple, he should at once be made a teacher, he would be lifted up into insolence. If before he had learned to be under rule, he should be appointed one of the rulers, he would be puffed up. Consequently, he adds, "Lest being lifted up with pride, he fall into the condemnation of the devil," that is, into the same condemnation which Satan incurred by his pride.

Verse 7. "Moreover he must have a good report of them which are outside of the church; lest he fall into reproach and the snare of the devil." This is rightly said, as he was certain to be reproached by them. Perhaps it was for the same reason that he said, "the husband of one wife," though elsewhere he says, "I would that all men were even as I myself," that is, practicing continence. That he may not therefore confine them within too narrow a limit, by requiring an over-strict conversation, he is satisfied to prescribe moderate virtue. For it was necessary to appoint one to preside in every city, as he writes to Titus, "That you should ordain elders in every city, as I had appointed you." But what if he should have a good report, and fair reputation, and not be worthy of it? In the first place this would not easily happen. It is much for good men to obtain a good report among their enemies. But, in fact, he has not left this to stand by itself; a good report "also," he says, that is, besides other qualities. What then, if they should speak evil of him without a cause from envy, especially as they were heathens? This was not to be expected. For even they will reverence a man of blameless life. Why then does he say, speaking of himself, "Through evil report and good report"? Because it was not his life that they assailed, but his preaching. Therefore he says, "through evil report." They were slandered as deceivers and impostors, on account of their preaching, and this because they could not attack their moral characters and lives. For why did no one say of the Apostles, that they were fornicators, unclean, or covetous persons, but that they were deceivers, which relates to their preaching only? Must it not be that their lives were irreproachable? It is abundantly clear.

Therefore, let us also live in such a way that no enemy or unbeliever will be able to speak evil of us. Even they revere the one whose life is virtuous. Truth stops the mouths even of enemies.

But how does he "fall into a snare"? By falling often into the same sins, as those who are outside of the church. If he is of such a character, the evil one soon lays another snare for him, and they soon effect his destruction. But if he should have a good report from his enemies, much more will he have it from his friends. We may infer from Christ's statement, "Let your light so shine before men, that they may see your good works, and glorify your Father which is in Heaven," that it is unlikely that the one living a blameless life would receive a bad report But what if one is falsely accused, and from peculiar circumstances be slandered? Well this is a possible case, but even that person should not be promoted. The result is much to be feared. Therefore it is said he should have "a good report," for your good works are to shine. As therefore no one will say that the sun is dark, not even the blind—for he will be ashamed to oppose the opinion of all—so him that is of remarkable goodness no one will blame. And though, on account of his doctrines, the Heathen will often slander him, yet they will not attack his virtuous life, but will join with others in admiring and revering it.

NPNF 1.13, ed. Philip Schaff. Reprint, Peabody, MA: Hendrickson, 1994.

John Chrysostom of Constantinople (347–407)
Homily Eleven on 1 Timothy

In this selection John speaks of the qualities of deacons and deaconesses. He also explains the difference between elders and bishops. The two offices had the same responsibilities; namely, teaching and presiding over the church.

The bishop, however, was distinguished from the presbyter only in the matter of ordination: the bishop had the authority to ordain and the elder did not. Other than this, he says, the duties were the same.

Having discussed Bishops and having described their character and the qualities which they ought to possess, and having passed over the order of Presbyters, he proceeds to that of Deacons. The reason of this omission was that there was no great difference between Presbyters and Bishops. Both had undertaken the office of Teachers and Presidents in the Church, and what he has said concerning Bishops is applicable to Presbyters. For they are only superior in having the power of ordination, and seem to have no other advantage over Presbyters.

"Likewise the Deacons." That is, they should have the same qualities as Bishops. And what are these same? To be blameless, sober, hospitable, patient, not brawlers, not covetous. And that he means this when he says "likewise" is evident from what he says in addition: "grave and not double-tongued," that is, not hollow or deceitful. Nothing so debases a man as deceit, nothing is so pernicious in the church as insincerity. "Not given to much wine, not greedy of filthy lucre; holding the mystery of the faith in a pure conscience." Thus he explains what he means by "blameless." And here he requires, though in other words, that he be "not a novice," where he says, "Let these also first be proved." The conjunction "also" is added to connect this with what had been said before of Bishops, for nothing intervenes between. And there is the same reason for the "not a novice" in that case. For would it not be absurd that a newly purchased slave is not entrusted with anything in a house until he has proven his character through the trial of time. This being so, why should one enter into the church of God from a state of heathenism and be at once placed in a station of preeminence?

Verse 11. "Even so must the women be grave, not slanderers, sober, faithful in all things."

Some have thought that this is said of women generally, but it is not so, for why should he introduce anything about women to interfere with his subject? He is speaking of those who hold the rank of Deaconesses.

Verse 12. "Let the Deacons be husbands of one wife." This must be understood therefore to relate to Deaconesses. For that order is necessary and useful and honorable in the church. Observe how he requires the same virtue from the Deacons, as from the Bishops, for though they were not of equal rank, they must equally be blameless; equally pure.

"Ruling their children and their own houses well."

Verse 13. "For they that have administered the office of a Deacon properly purchase to themselves a good degree, and much boldness in the faith which is in Christ Jesus."

Everywhere they are required to rule their children well in order that others may not be scandalized by their misconduct.

"They that administer the office of a Deacon properly purchase to themselves a good degree," that is, advancement, "and much boldness in the faith of Jesus Christ." This is as if he would say that those who have been found vigilant in the lower degree will soon ascend to the higher.

Verses 14, 15. "These things write I unto you, hoping to come unto you shortly. But if I tarry long, that you may know how you ought to behave yourself in the house of God, which is the church of the living God, the pillar and ground of the truth."

That he may not plunge Timothy into dejection by giving him orders about such matters, he says, I write this way not as though I were not coming, but I will indeed come, still in case I should be delayed, that you may not be distressed. And this he writes to him to prevent him from becoming dejected, but to others in order to rouse them to greater earnestness.

NPNF 1.13, ed. Philip Schaff. Reprint, Peabody, MA: Hendrickson, 1994.

ADDITIONAL READINGS

Campenhausen, H. von. *Ecclesiastical Authority and Spiritual Power in the Church of the First Three Centuries*, tr. J. A. Baker. Stanford: Stanford University Press, 1969.

Culbertson, P. L. and A. B. Shippee, eds., *The Pastor: Readings from the Patristic Period*. Minneapolis: Fortress, 1990.

Cunningham, A. *The Bishop in the Church: Patristic Texts on the Role of the* Episkopos. Wilmington, DE: Glazier, 1985.

Ferguson, E., ed. *Church, Ministry, and Organization in the Early Church Era*, Studies in Early Christianity, vol. 13. New York: Garland, 1993.

Ferguson, E., ed. *Women in Early Christianity*, Studies in Early Christianity, vol 14. New York: Garland, 1993.

Harnack, A. von. *The Constitution and Law of the Church in the First Two Centuries*. London: Norgate and Williams, 1910.

Hatch, E. *The Organization of the Early Christian Churches*. London: Rivingtons, 1888.

Lindsay, T. M. *The Church and the Ministry in the Early Centuries.* London: Hodder and Stoughton, 1902.

Swete, H. B., ed. *Essays on the Early History of the Church and the Ministry.* London: Macmillan, 1918.

Torjensen, K. J. *When Women Were Priests: Women's Leadership in the Early Church and the Scandal of Their Subordination in the Rise of Christianity.* San Francisco: HarperCollins, 1995.

Notes

Note to the Introduction

1. The term "patristic" is from the Latin *pater*, meaning father. The patristic period refers to the time of the "Church Fathers," extending from the middle of the first century to the end of the sixth century.

Notes to Chapter 1

1. The Lord's Supper is the subject of chapter 4, "Uniting the Community."
2. Matthew 28:18–20.
3. See chapter 2, "Assembling the Community."
4. *Eusebius of Caesanea, Church History* 3.25.4. NPNF 2.1, ed. W. Sanday. Reprint, Peabody, MA: Hendrickson, 1994.
5. *Athanasius of Alexandria, Festal Letter* 39. NPNF 2.4, ed. W. Sanday. Reprint, Peabody, MA: Hendrickson, 1994.
6. Matthew 28:18–20.
7. For the different offices, and their roles, see chapter 6, "Leading the Community."

Notes to Chapter 3

1. See chapter 6, "Leading the Community."
2. See ibid.
3. See chapter 5, "Expanding the Community."

Note to Chapter 4

1. Docetism is the title for this conception of the Incarnation. It comes from the word for "seeming."

Index

About the Editor

Steven A. McKinion is currently Associate Professor of Church History at the Southeastern Baptist Theological Seminary in Wake Forest, North Carolina, where he has taught since 1998. Dr. McKinion teaches courses on general church history as well as historical theology. His specialty is early Christian doctrine and practice, and he has written on topics ranging from Christology (the doctrine of the person of Jesus Christ) to the Christian interpretation of the Bible.

Dr. McKinion holds a B.A. from Mississippi College, an M.A. from the University of Mobile, and a Ph.D. from the University of Aberdeen, Scotland. He is an ordained Southern Baptist minister, and has served churches in different ministerial capacities. He and his wife Ginger have two young children, Lachlan and Blakely.